Fri

Someone placed a smelly blanket over Jody's head, and strong arms grabbed her from behind. She tried to yell, but the blanket muffled her cries. She struggled, but she could feel something soft, like a bunched-up sheet, being wrapped around the blanket, effectively pinning her arms to her sides so that she couldn't move. Whoever had attacked her moved quickly and efficiently.

Jody felt herself being picked up and carried down the stairs. She heard a door being opened, and she felt herself being lowered to the ground. Then she heard a door slam shut. She yelled for help, but she knew that no one could hear her shouts. She knew that she was all alone . . .

Jody fought back despair and hysterics. *If I am being kidnapped*, she thought, *Mom and Jake will get me out.* Yet deep inside Jody knew that this wasn't an ordinary kidnapping. She had been trussed up like a turkey because someone wanted her out of the way . . .

And that someone had to be connected with the concert.

The first Jody and Jake Mystery

Also by the same author, and available in Knight Books:

The Case of the Counterfeit Racehorse
The Case of the Fire-Raising Gang

The Case of the Frightened Rock Star

A Jody and Jake Mystery

Elizabeth Levy

KNIGHT BOOKS
Hodder and Stoughton

First published in the United States of America in 1980 by Pocket Books, a Simon & Schuster division of Gulf & Western Corporation, New York.

First published in Great Britain by Knight Books in 1982
Second impression 1982

British Library C.I.P.

Levy, Elizabeth
The case of the Frightened Rock Star
(Knight
books)
I. Title
813'.54[J] PZ7

ISBN 0-340-28332-7

The characters and situations in this book are entirely imaginary and bear no relation to any real person or actual happening

Printed and bound in Great Britain for Hodder and Stoughton Paperbacks, a division of Hodder and Stoughton Ltd, Mill Road, Dunton Green, Sevenoaks, Kent (Editorial Office: 47 Bedford Square, London, WC1 3DP) by Cox & Wyman Ltd, Reading. Photoset by Rowland Phototypesetting Ltd, Bury St Edmunds, Suffolk.

CONTENTS

1

CHEWING GUM ON THE DOORKNOB

Jody Markson put her hand on the doorknob and instantly tried to pull it away. It stuck. 'Yuk!' she exclaimed, examining the gooey chewing gum that clung to her palm.

'Jake!' she screamed. Her brother came running to the front door. His longish curly red hair bobbed around his face. Harpo, the Markson's dog which had the curly black hair of a poodle and the floppy ears of a spaniel, joined Jake at the door, wagging his tail furiously at the sight of Jody. Jody had brought Harpo home from the pound just three months ago, but he loved her as if he had known her all his life. Nobody knew how old Harpo was, and he would probably have been put to sleep because no one else had wanted him. For the moment, Jody ignored him and turned to Jake.

'Did you do that?' asked Jody angrily, waving her hand in Jake's face. 'That's the dumbest joke in the book.'

Jake watched his sister try to pull the chewing gum from her hand. He smiled.

'I didn't do it,' he protested. 'I bet it was one of the neighbour's kids. You know that's not my style.'

'I bet,' said Jody. She looked down at the big piece of cardboard she had been carrying. 'Will you pick up the poster for me? I don't want to get chewing gum on it.' She walked into the house, shaking her long brown hair out of her face because she didn't want to touch her hair with her sticky hand. Harpo leaped up and down by her side. 'I see you,' said Jody, smiling. 'I just can't touch you until I get this stupid gum off my hand.'

As she stood in the bathroom, trying to wash the chewing gum off her hand, Jody had to admit that putting gum on the doorknob did not seem like something Jake would do. Jody had just turned fifteen. Jake was only a year younger. He could be immature at times, thought Jody, but not that immature. She walked back into the living room, convinced that Jake had been right. One of the little kids in the neighbourhood had probably done it.

Jake had propped the cardboard poster up on the dining room table. He looked at it critically. It announced that Michael Harper would return to Shady Brook High School for his first concert in his home town, a benefit to rebuild the high school stadium, which had burned down when he was a senior.

'Don't you like it?' Jody asked. 'We just picked them up from the printer today.' Jody sounded anxious. She was the one responsible for bringing Michael Harper back to his home town, and if the concert was a bust, it would be her fault.

'The poster's fine,' said Jake. 'It's the face.'

'What's wrong with his face?' Jody stared at the smiling face on the poster, almost too innocent looking to be a rock star.

'He looks too sweet,' said Jake as if he could read his sister's mind. 'He looks almost as gooey as the music he's been writing lately. I loved "The Joke's on Me".' 'The Joke's on Me' had been Michael Harper's first and only hit.

'His new songs haven't been so bad,' said Jody defensively.

'Well, I bet you're the only one who's played them,' said Jake. 'Don't you wish we had been at the stadium the first time anybody heard "The Joke's on Me"?'

'We could have been killed,' said Jody. 'That's the night the stadium burned to the ground, remember?'

'Yeah,' said Jake. 'But you have to admit, it was a terrific joke. I just wish I could have been there.'

'Maybe we could recreate it for the concert,' said Jody dryly.

'Great idea,' said Jake. 'I'll put on a wig and play the principal's wife.' Jake pretended to grab a microphone, and he sang falsetto: 'Oh . . . say can you see . . .'

'Don't forget to sing, "Grapefruit through the night",' said Jody, laughing. 'She always sings "Gave proof through the night" so that it sounds like "grapefruit".'

At the annual homecoming game between Shady Brook and Grover Cleveland, the principal's wife always sang 'The Star-Spangled Banner'. She had studied opera and she thought she had a wonderful voice. She didn't.

Jake continued singing in such a high voice that Harpo's ears twitched back and forth.

'Careful,' warned Jody. 'I think Harpo's going to howl.'

Jake stopped singing and patted Harpo on the head. 'It's okay, Harpo.' Jake turned to Jody. 'Who do you think got the idea to fix the microphones?' he asked.

'Nobody ever found out,' said Jody. 'Apparently, the principal's wife stepped up to the mike, opened her mouth, and "The Joke's on Me" blared out through the microphone. A lot of people thought Michael did it himself, or else his friend Tommy Montag, who used to sing with him. I don't think they ever proved who did it.'

'I heard that Michael Harper was on the field, and the other players swore he looked shocked when he heard his voice bounce off the stadium walls,' said Jake.

'It must have been funny,' said Jody. 'It would have gone down as one of the great practical jokes of all time if it hadn't backfired.'

'Backfired is the right word,' said Jake. 'I remember near the end of the song there was a sudden crackling noise and the principal and his wife smelled the smoke first. Luckily, the principal had such a loud voice that even without a microphone he could be heard. He yelled "Fire!" Everyone got out of the stadium and no one was hurt.'

'Did they ever question Tommy Montag?' Jody asked.

'They didn't have a chance,' said Jake. 'He ran away the next day. He hasn't been heard from since.'

'I wonder if Michael Harper feels strange about coming home,' mused Jody. 'I still can't believe he answered my letter.'

Soon after his graduation, Michael Harper had recorded 'The Joke's on Me' and it became an instant hit. He had moved to California and had never returned. In the meantime, the stadium remained a burned-out shell. There were simply no funds to rebuild it. Each year the students at Shady Brook had tried various fund-raising events, everything from cake sales to lotteries, but no real money had come in.

Then two months ago, Jody had got the idea of writing to Michael Harper and ask him for help. All her friends had laughed at her, and nobody had expected him to answer. After he had become famous, he had seemed to think he was too good for his home town, and many people had tried to lure him back, but he had always refused.

'Something about your letter must have gotten to him,' said Jake.

'I just wrote him about how depressing it was to have to walk by the empty hulk of the stadium every day,' said Jody.

'Well, it must have been some letter,' said Jake. 'Now, you're in charge of the concert.'

'I can't believe how much work it is,' said Jody. She looked worried. 'I just hope that everything goes okay.'

2

CRYING OVER SPILLED PAINT

Michael Harper and his manager had arrived in town and called her. Jody planned to show them the posters the next day. She glanced at the poster, fresh from the printer, and she looked worried.

'It's the Markson luck,' said Jake. 'You're the chairman of the concert, and you've got a has-been rock star on your hands.'

'Chairperson,' said Jody automatically.

'Right. I'm glad Mom didn't hear me.' Mrs Markson was a criminal lawyer. She and Mr Markson had been divorced several years ago. Mr Markson was a psychologist in New York, and sometimes Jody and Jake visited him during the summer. Both their parents had raised Jody and Jake to be independent. They were used to taking care of themselves. Several times, Jody and Jake had become involved in investigations of Mrs Markson's cases.

'Is Mom coming home for dinner?' asked Jody.

'I think she's working late,' said Jake. 'Now, excuse me. The co-person has to begin dinner. It's my turn to cook tonight.' Jake walked into the kitchen. Jody followed him, carrying the poster and frowning.

'Do you really think the concert is going to be a bust?' she asked, sounding worried.

'No,' said Jake. He grabbed a banana. 'People are curious to see Michael Harper return to his home town. You'll sell some tickets.'

'I don't want to sell *some* tickets. I want a sell-out!'

'Naturally,' said Jake, taking a bite of the banana.

'I want you to make sure that all your friends sell a lot of tickets,' ordered Jody.

'Yes, ma'am,' said Jake, giving his sister a mock salute.

'This isn't funny. We've rented Vickers Stadium. It holds 9,000. What if we give the concert, and only a handful of people show up?'

'That won't happen,' said Jake. 'We're bound to have enough to make two teams. We can play football.'

'Jake! I'm serious.'

'What do you want me to do about it? Maybe he'll start writing good songs again.'

'You've got me worried,' said Jody. 'Why do you think he's been writing such dumb songs lately?'

'Ah-ha, even you admit they're dumb.'

'Yeah, but his first song was great,' insisted Jody.

'Who knows?' Jake shrugged his shoulders.

'Maybe once he got rich, he got lazy. Maybe he had only one good song in him.' Jake looked at the poster of Michael Harper again. 'He doesn't look very smart.'

'He got good grades when he went to high school.'

'That doesn't mean much,' said Jake. 'Look at you. You get all A's.'

'Very funny,' said Jody. 'You could get good grades, too, if you weren't such a goof-off.'

'Jake does not live up to his potential,' said Jake, speaking in a mincing, mocking tone, perfectly imitating the voice of a report card, if a report card could speak. 'How many times do you think I've had that written on my report card?' he asked.

'Two thousand,' answered Jody. 'I think it was written on

your wrist tag when Mom had you in the hospital.'

Jake laughed. 'Yeah, you probably wrote it.'

'No, I didn't start to write until I was four and a half, and I was only fourteen months old when you were born,' said Jody seriously.

Jake glanced at his sister. 'I was kidding,' he said.

'Oh,' said Jody, sounding preoccupied. 'I'm going to hate it if this concert isn't a smash.'

'You certainly have a one-track mind,' said Jake. 'It won't be a bust, not with the great Jody Markson in charge.'

'But it could be. I bet a lot of kids feel like you do.'

'Well, you've got to admit, it's kind of embarrassing when the most famous rock star to come out of your high school turns out to be a has-been at nineteen.'

'I've got an idea that might make this concert work.'

'How about hiring another rock star?' suggested Jake. Jody gave him a dirty look. 'Okay, I take that back,' said Jake. 'What's your great idea?'

'You gave it to me when you said how much you wished you had been there when the stadium burned down.'

'You're actually going to re-create the burning of the stadium!' said Jake incredulously.

'No, don't be silly. But people are curious about what Michael was like before he became a star. I thought maybe we could get some kids at school to put on a short pageant about Michael Harper and his life at Shady Brook. After all, it's a benefit for the high school. We'd put on a whole history of Michael Harper's days at Shady Brook. It could be funny and sentimental – "A Rock Star Comes Back to Remember His High School and Help It Out". I think I could get some good press coverage, and TV, too.'

Jake looked sceptical. 'Michael Harper may not want you digging up his past,' warned Jake. 'They never did find out exactly who was responsible for the fire.'

Jake began to rummage through the refrigerator. He was by far the best cook in the family. Jody was practically hopeless in the kitchen. She could follow recipes exactly, but the food seemed to sense that she didn't care about it, and nothing came out quite right.

Jake loved to cook. He had started to cook when he was in the fourth grade, specialising in macaroni cheese and chocolate pudding. Now, he made all kinds of spaghetti with different sauces. Mrs Markson often complained that he was a mixed blessing. She loved having a son who cooked, but she got fat. Jake called himself the spaghetti king, but he never gained weight because he was a runner. Jody just never gained weight without doing anything. Everyone was jealous because Jody had one of those metabolisms that allowed her to eat whatever she wanted without ever putting on weight. So poor Mrs Markson was the only one with a problem, and she loved Jake's spaghetti too much to ever give it up for a diet.

'What are we having tonight?' asked Jody. She was perched on a stool by the counter, watching Jake cook. Groucho and Chico, two cats Jody had also rescued from the pound, jumped up on the counter and demanded to be petted. Jody planned on being a veterinary surgeon when she grew up, and she had a wonderful way with animals. She worked as a volunteer at the pound, and if she could have had her way, the Markson's house would be overrun with animals. However, Mrs Markson had drawn the line at two cats and one dog.

Jake held out his hand and gave Chico and Groucho each a bit of minced clam. 'We're having spaghetti with clam sauce,' he said.

The phone rang. Jody picked it up. Nobody was there. She put down the receiver. 'I wonder what rock stars eat,' she said.

'I think they like junk food,' said Jake. 'You can ask Michael when you meet him tomorrow.'

Jody looked disdainfully at the ingredients on the kitchen counter. Groucho and Chico each stole another bit of clam.

'There's nothing much to nibble on with this recipe,' she said, complaining.

'The cats like it,' said Jake. He started to chop some garlic. 'Have some garlic. It keeps the vampires away.'

'I haven't met any vampires lately.'

'That's because I always feed you garlic,' said Jake. 'Besides, you never know when you're going to meet a vampire.'

The phone rang again.

'Hello!' said Jody sharply. She put the receiver back down. 'Someone has called twice and hung up,' she said to Jake.

'It's probably the same kid who put chewing gum on the door,' said Jake.

'It's very annoying. What were we talking about?'

'Vampires,' said Jake. The phone rang again. 'I'll get it this time. Maybe it's one of my secret admirers, and she doesn't want to talk to you.' Jake picked up the phone. 'It's for you,' he said, handing the phone to his sister. Jody looked at him quizzically. She put her ear to the receiver.

'Is this your idea of a joke?' she demanded.

'What do you mean?'

'There's nobody there,' said Jody. 'I'm beginning to think you put the chewing gum on the door, after all.'

'I swear,' said Jake, 'a male voice asked to speak to Jody Markson.'

'And then hung up,' said Jody sarcastically. 'Is this some joke you and your friends thought up?'

'No,' insisted Jake. 'Somebody's just playing a joke on you. Forget it.'

Jody gave the phone a dirty look, as if her look could be transmitted through the wires. 'I definitely think practical jokes are the lowest form of humour,' she said.

'Most people say puns are the lowest form of humour,' said Jake.

'Puns don't get gum on your hands,' said Jody. The phone rang again. 'I'll get it,' said Jody, picking up the receiver.

'Now listen!' she yelled. 'You stop calling . . . oh . . . I'm sorry . . .' Jody listened into the phone.

Jake grinned. He wondered who had been the innocent victim of Jody's tirade. Jody hung up the phone looking very upset.

'That was Robie,' said Jody. Robie was one of Jody's best friends. She was on Jody's committee to co-ordinate the work for the concert.

'She must have thought you were a nut when you started yelling at her,' said Jake.

'She was too upset to notice. We've had a catastrophe.'

'What's wrong?' asked Jake anxiously. Jody looked furious.

'Robie was at school. She stayed late for track practice. She went into the supply closet to take one of the posters home, the way I did, and found that someone had spilled red paint on all our posters. They're ruined.'

'You're kidding!' said Jake.

'No,' moaned Jody. 'And those posters cost a lot of money. The school advanced it to us, but they don't have any more. We don't have any money for new ones. I don't know what we're going to do.'

Jake looked sympathetic. 'Maybe Michael Harper will pay the additional printing costs,' he suggested. 'Why don't you call him? Do you know how to reach him?'

Jody looked indecisive. 'I hate to talk to him about a foul-up the first time I meet him. It's so embarrassing.'

'It wasn't your fault.'

'I know, but he's a rock star. I hate to bother him with these petty details. He's doing us enough of a favour by just showing up.'

'*Was* a rock star, remember? Besides, he must have so much money from his first hit, the cost of reprinting the posters will be nothing to him.'

'I guess you're right,' said Jody tentatively. 'I could kill the goof-off who spilled the paint.'

'No use crying over spilled paint,' said Jake cheerfully. Jody threw a piece of parsley at him.

'Why is there a parsley fight going on in my kitchen?' asked Mrs Markson, putting down her briefcase. She was a beautiful woman with dark blonde hair and strong features.

Jody jumped up off the stool and gave her mother a kiss. 'Jake said you weren't coming home for dinner.'

'My trial got postponed.' She walked around the kitchen counter and gave Jake a kiss. 'I'm on a diet,' she announced. Jody and Jake exchanged glances. Mrs Markson announced she was on a diet at least once a day.

'Who's that?' asked Mrs Markson, pointing to the poster leaning against the kitchen cabinets.

'Mom,' said Jody, 'that's Michael Harper.'

'Be careful of that poster,' said Jake. 'It may be worth a lot of money someday. It's the only one in existence.'

'So that's the Michael Harper of Jody's concert,' said Mrs Markson.

'It's not my concert,' said Jody indignantly.

'Well, you've hardly talked about anything else since you wrote that letter,' said Mrs Markson. 'And you and Robie have never worked so hard.' Mrs Markson looked at the poster. 'He looks very bland for a rock star.'

'I don't think you should make insulting remarks about his looks when you haven't even met him,' complained Jody.

'I'm sorry,' said her mother, sounding surprised. 'I didn't mean to be personal. I didn't realise you'd be so touchy. Will we get to meet him? I've never met a rock star.'

'You'd better ask him for his autograph quick before Jody asks him to pay the printer's bill,' said Jake.

'Oh, just shut up, will you?' said Jody. 'I'm going to go call him.' She stalked out of the kitchen.

'What's wrong with her?' asked Mrs Markson.

'She's had a tough day,' said Jake. 'Chewing gum on the doorknob, paint on her posters; it takes a lot out of a person.'

Mrs Markson gave her son a perplexed look.

3

A NERVOUS ROCK STAR

Jake was about to put the spaghetti into the boiling water when Jody came back to the kitchen smiling.

'I talked to him!' she said excitedly. 'He said he would have to put in a call to his manager, but that he'd be glad to pay for the reprinting. He was really sympathetic.'

'Why does he have to call his manager to write one lousy cheque?' asked Jake.

'I don't know,' said Jody. 'I guess his manager takes care of all his money. Anyhow, I haven't told you the really exciting part.'

'Okay, what's the really exciting part?'

'He's coming over here tonight.'

'Here!?'

'Yes. He said he had some questions he wanted to talk to me about.'

'Is he coming for dinner?' asked Jake nervously.

'No, afterwards,' said Jody.

'Good,' said Jake. 'I never cooked for a rock star before.'

They were just finishing the spaghetti when the doorbell rang. For several seconds, nobody moved. It was almost a family tradition to argue about who would get the door.

'Isn't that your rock star?' asked Mrs Markson.

'He's not my rock star,' said Jody.

'I only meant, is anybody going to get the door, or should I get it?' said Mrs Markson. 'We're an intelligent family. You'd think we'd work out a system for answering the door.'

'Do you want me to get it?' asked Jake.

The doorbell rang again.

'This is stupid!' shouted Jody, and she ran for the door.

'She's so tense,' commented Mrs Markson.

'It's the concert,' said Jake. 'She's nervous. It was all her idea, after all.'

Jody entered with a thin-looking young man with dark circles under his eyes. He looked much less boyish in person than in his pictures.

'Mom, Jake, I want you to meet Michael Harper,' said Jody.

Michael's eyes darted around the dining room. He glanced at his picture on the poster, then quickly looked away.

'Have you had any dinner?' asked Mrs Markson. 'Jake, do you have any spaghetti left?'

'I'm not hungry,' said Michael.

'If you haven't had any dinner, you're missing a treat,' said Mrs Markson. 'I'm not bragging. Jake made it.'

Michael glanced at Jake. He was nervously playing with a lock of his hair. *He's frightened*, thought Jake. *He looks like a scared deer.*

'Well, if it's not too much trouble,' said Michael. 'I guess I could use some carbos.'

'Carbos?' said Jake, recognising the runner's slang for carbohydrates. Runners believe that carbohydrates, like pasta and bread, are good for them because they are the easiest fuel for a body to turn into energy, and runners need tremendous amounts of energy. 'Do you run?' Jake asked.

'Yeah,' said Michael. 'It's the only thing that cleans my head out.'

'I run, too,' said Jake. 'Maybe while you're in town we can run together.'

'Sure,' muttered Michael. Jake felt awkward, as if Michael thought he was just a kid wanting to hang around a rock star. Jake walked into the kitchen and brought out a plate of spaghetti with clam sauce.

'I can heat it up if it needs it,' said Jake, placing the food in front of Michael.

'No, its fine,' mumbled Michael. 'Thanks.' His eyes kept glancing around the dining room nervously.

'How much do you run?' asked Jake.

'About forty miles a week,' answered Michael. Jake looked at him with new respect. Obviously, Michael was a real runner. Runners almost never talked about how much they ran in a day, but added up their mileage for a week, since the best training was to vary the number of miles a day – hard one day, easy the next.

'If you'll excuse me,' said Mrs Markson, 'I'm going to my study to work.' She smiled. 'If you'll forgive me, Michael, I'm afraid that I think running would be the most boring thing in the world if it didn't run a distant second to talking about running.'

'I understand,' said Michael. 'It's boring if you don't run yourself.'

'It's nice to meet you,' said Mrs Markson. 'Good luck with your concert.' She left the room.

'Do you write songs in your head as you run?' Jody asked.

'No,' said Michael bitterly. He twisted his hair again nervously. 'I try to write songs out of my head.'

'Huh?' said Jody. 'I don't understand.'

'Well, you wouldn't,' said Michael. Jody looked hurt. Michael glanced up from his spaghetti and seemed to take them in as people for the first time.

'Hey, I'm sorry,' he said. 'I didn't mean that the way it sounded.'

'It's okay,' said Jody.

'Look,' said Michael, 'you have to understand your letter made me very nervous.' He smiled and for the first time Jody saw some of the charm that she had seen on television when Michael first became a star.

'My letter?' asked Jody. 'You mean the one I wrote about doing the benefit for the stadium?'

'Yeah,' said Michael. 'It's not often that I'm shook up by letters from fifteen-year-old girls. No offence meant,' he added quickly. 'But when I saw the postmark, I almost flipped . . . I thought . . .' Michael's voice trailed off.

Chico jumped up on his lap and Michael patted him absent-mindedly. Harpo lay by Jody's feet, and Groucho was sleeping in between Harpo's paws.

'They're great animals,' said Michael. 'I thought cats and dogs don't get along.'

'They can be easily taught, especially in a home,' said Jody. 'We just had to teach Harpo that Chico and Groucho weren't here for him to eat.'

'Jody can teach any animal anything,' bragged Jake. 'If she had her way, every stray animal would find a home here. Mom puts a limit on her.'

Michael scratched Chico behind the ears and Chico purred contentedly. Groucho woke up and jumped onto Michael's lap, nudging Chico aside in order to demand his share of Michael's attention.

Michael laughed. 'Chico, Harpo, and Groucho . . . Aren't there supposed to be four Marx brothers? Where's Zeppo?'

'Mom says three animals plus us equals the best of the Marx brothers' routines,' said Jody. She looked at Michael curiously. He seemed almost to be stalling for time.

'What were the questions you wanted to ask me?' Jody asked, always in favour of the most direct approach.

Michael seemed to shake himself. He startled Groucho, who jumped off his lap, landing on Harpo, who turned around and playfully batted at Groucho with his paw. Michael stared at them. 'They seem like such good friends,' he said.

'I told you, they are,' said Jody.

'Exactly why did you write that letter?' Michael blurted out.

Jody blushed. 'One day my friend Robie and I were talking about how sad it was that we would have to go through all our high school years without a stadium. Robie runs the hurdles. She was saying that no one comes to watch the track meets because they have to use the old Vickers Stadium in the middle of the town. That's where we have the football games, and that's where we're having the concert, but it's a drag to get there. It's a long way from school, and a lot of kids don't bother.

'Anyhow, we were talking about ways we could raise money, and all of a sudden I thought about writing to you. Robie bet me that you would never answer, and I won that bet.'

'Nobody put you up to it?' asked Michael thoughtfully.

'No. What do you mean?' asked Jody.

'Nothing. It was a good letter. It brought back a lot of memories.' Michael played with his hair nervously. 'You were right. It was time for me to come back home. That's what you wrote in your letter.'

Jody blushed again. Jake had never seen her blush so much, but then he realised that he had never seen her with someone famous before, either.

Michael seemed lost in thought. Jody glanced at her brother. There was something extremely odd going on, but she couldn't understand what it was. Michael seemed to want some information from her, but for the life of her, she couldn't imagine what he wanted.

Michael gave himself that strange little shake, as he had done earlier. 'I couldn't get hold of my manager to tell him about your problem with the posters, so I wrote you a cheque myself. I'm sure it's good.'

'Thanks,' said Jody, smiling. 'I've got such great plans. I know I can make this concert a success.'

'You've never seen my sister when she's determined,' said

Jake. 'She's already got the local radio and TV stations to broadcast free announcements about the concert. They've been on the air all week.' For some reason Jake's news seemed to make Michael even more nervous.

'And I'm sure we can get even more publicity,' said Jody. 'People love sentimental stories, and if we tell them we're putting on a pageant about your days at Shady Brook . . .'

'I'm not sure that's such a great idea,' mumbled Michael. He gave an almost savage tug to his lock of hair, and then he fell silent.

'I think I'll make some coffee,' said Jody. 'Jake will you help me?'

'You make lousy coffee,' said Jake. 'You never make coffee.'

Jody could have kicked him. 'I think Michael needs some, or wants some,' said Jody. Michael looked almost as if he had forgotten where he was. Jody raised her eyebrows and gestured toward the kitchen.

'Yes,' repeated Jody. 'Please come into the kitchen and help me.' Jody turned to Michael. 'We'll be right back.'

Jody closed the door behind her.

'You are the biggest dolt in the world,' said Jody. 'I wanted to talk to you alone; I didn't just want to make coffee.'

'I realised that,' said Jake. 'I was just a little slow.'

'I agree with that,' said Jody, deadpan. Then she looked serious. 'Jake will you help me?'

'You make lousy coffee,' said Jake. What do you think is wrong with him? Doesn't he strike you as odd?'

'He's all wired up.'

'Do you think he takes drugs?' Jody asked. 'He makes me nervous, especially the way he plays with his hair.'

'I don't know,' answered Jake. 'It's hard to imagine anybody running forty miles a week *and* taking drugs.'

'It's hard to imagine anybody running forty miles a week, period,' said Jody. She found running almost as boring as her mother did. Jody occasionally accompanied Jake on a run, only because she thought it was good for her. Jake, on the other hand, genuinely loved to run. Jody couldn't understand it.

'You know,' said Jake, 'I think we should make some coffee. Otherwise, he's going to be suspicious.'

'You make it,' said Jody absent-mindedly.

Jake smiled ruefully. 'Someday you're going to give the wrong person orders, and you're going to be sorry.'

'I didn't mean to order you around,' said Jody. 'I apologise. It's just that I thought Michael Harper would be a lot different.'

'Your hero,' said Jake sarcastically.

'He's sort of nice, said Jody. 'The animals like him, only he's so serious. If he's on drugs, he'll never give a good concert.'

'I don't think drugs are his problem,' said Jake. 'I think he's just very nervous about coming back to his home town, especially now that he's not such a big star anymore. Remember, he really only had that one hit.'

'Don't keep reminding me,' said Jody. 'I'm in big trouble if this concert flops. The school had to lay out a lot of money in advance. We had to pay for the stadium. The cheque from Michael will help, but it's just a drop in the bucket.'

'Stop worrying,' said Jake. 'You're going to have a great concert. Come on. We'd better go in and give him coffee.'

Michael was sitting where they had left him, surrounded by Chico, Harpo, and Groucho. He stroked Harpo gently with his foot, while Chico and Groucho each got a hand.

'They look like they've got you occupied,' said Jake.

'Yeah,' said Michael. 'I feel like I'm a one-man band. Look, I've got to get going.' He reached into his pocket and pulled out a cheque.

'Here's the cheque for the posters,' said Michael. 'I didn't know how much it would cost, so I left the amount blank.'

Jody looked shocked. She helped her mother keep the accounts, and she knew that if you gave a person a blank cheque, he or she could fill it for any amount and wipe out your entire bank account. 'You shouldn't have done that,' said Jody. 'I'll try to find out how much it should be.'

'Don't worry about it,' said Michael. 'I never worry about money. My manager keeps all my books. Just fill it in when you go to the printer's. He may charge you extra because it's a rush job.'

'Thanks,' said Jody. She folded the cheque carefully and put it in her wallet. 'Are you sure you don't want to fill it in?'

Michael pulled nervously at his hair again. 'I told you I never pay any attention to money. I just wanted to come over here and find out whether anybody put you up to writing that letter.'

Jody shook her head no. 'What about my idea for the pageant?' she asked.

'I'll be in touch about that,' said Michael. He walked to the door. All three animals seemed sad to see him go.

4

THE BODY IN THE DITCH

'You mean you got to meet Michael Harper, and you didn't even call me?' shrieked Robie. They were standing outside school before classes.

'You'll get to meet him,' said Jody. 'Jake talked me into calling him right away and asking him for money to reprint the posters.'

'What was he like?' Robie asked, looking up at Jody. She was a good four inches shorter than Jody's five feet six inches, and Robie often joked that it was her misfortune to pick the tallest girl in the class as her best friend. Jody teased Robie back by telling her she jumped hurdles just to see what it felt like to be tall for a few seconds at a time. They had been good friends since the fourth grade. Robie wrapped her chain around her bike. 'Come on, tell me what he was like,' she insisted.

'He was weird,' said Jody. 'I wish you had been there. The only thing he was interested in was who gave me the idea of writing to him. He seemed suspicious, and his mind kept wandering.'

'Maybe he takes drugs,' Robie suggested.

'That's what I thought,' said Jody. 'But he runs forty miles a week. Jake said he didn't think anybody could do that and still take drugs.'

'I agree,' said Robie. 'Besides, he gave you the cheque for the printer. That's what's important.'

'How did the accident happen, anyhow?' Jody asked.

'I don't know. I stayed late in the gym to do some exercises with weights, and then I decided to get one of the posters and bring it home to show my parents.'

Jody nodded. 'That was fine. That's what I did.'

'I know, but when I turned the light on in the supply cabinet, there was sticky red paint all over the posters.'

'So the paint hadn't dried yet,' said Jody.

'No, the paint was wet,' answered Robie. 'There was a bottle of red paint on the shelf above the posters. Somebody must have left the top loose and it spilled by accident. I felt awful.'

'It wasn't your fault,' said Jody. 'Let's just hope that's the worst foul-up with the concert. Do you want to go to the printer's with me after school?'

'Gee,' said Robie, with a grin, 'you invite me to go along for all the exciting stuff.'

'I promise you, you'll meet Michael Harper. Besides, I want to find out what you think of him.'

'Okay, I'll go to the printer's with you.'

'Great,' said Jody.

After school, they got on their bikes and headed for the printer's, whose plant was on the edge of town. Jody tucked her purse into her front basket. Her back carrier had been broken for weeks. She kept meaning to have it fixed, but she hadn't gotten around to it. Jody was a straight-A student, and great with animals, but she wasn't good at fixing things. Neither was Jake nor Mrs Markson, for that matter.

Robie carried her stuff around in a knapsack, which she carried on her back. Robie was a stronger bike rider than Jody, but she held back so they could ride at a leisurely, comfortable pace. They were only a couple of miles from the printer's when suddenly Jody gasped.

She stared at the side of the road in dismay. A man was

lying face down in the ditch by the side of the road. He wasn't moving.

'Look!' exclaimed Jody. She and Robie quickly braked their bicycles over to the shoulder and jumped off, leaving their bikes out of the traffic's way on the side of the road. They ran to the man. Robie got to the ditch first. She went to the man and turned him over to see if he was all right. She screamed. Jody stared. It was nothing but a suit of clothes stuffed with newspapers to look like a body. A hat had been placed where the head should be. Jody heard the sound of a car starting up on the road. She scrambled out of the ditch and looked around. The road was empty.

'What a sick joke!' exclaimed Jody.

'It's disgusting,' said Robie. 'I really thought it was a body.'

'Me, too,' said Jody.

'Whoever did that has a sick mind,' said Robie. She peered into the woods by the side of the road. 'I bet they're hiding around here somewhere. They probably got a big kick out of hearing me scream. I hate practical jokes.'

'There's been an epidemic of them recently,' said Jody. 'I hope they don't come in threes.'

'What do you mean?' asked Robie. Jody told her about the chewing gum.

'Compared to stuffing old clothes to make them look like a body, chewing gum now seems like an innocent joke,' said Jody.

'I know,' said Robie. 'This joke could have easily caused an accident if there had been more traffic or if we had been driving a car.'

Furiously, Jody pulled the newspapers out of the suit of clothes. 'We're not leaving it around to scare anybody else,' she said. She rolled the clothes into a ball and stuck them under a log.

'Come on,' said Jody. 'We've got to get to the printer's before he closes.' They climbed out of the ditch. Their bikes were just where they had left them. They got back on their bikes and made it to the printer's without further incident.

They told the printer about finding the fake body by the road. 'It's a sick world,' said the printer, Mr Mitford. 'I bet it was the same bunch of crazy fools who spilled paint all over your posters. Malicious little monsters. I don't know what gets into you kids today.'

Jody hated it when adults lumped all kids together into one easy generalisation. 'You don't know that it was kids,' said Jody indignantly. 'There are a lot of sick adults around, too.' Robie nodded her head in agreement.

Mr Mitford looked at them suspiciously. 'I don't know about that,' he said.

'Anyhow,' said Jody, 'I've brought you a cheque to cover the cost of re-doing the posters. It's a rush job. If we don't have those posters soon, we might as well not bother with the concert.'

'That might be a good idea,' said Mr Mitford cantankerously. 'I think maybe it's that rock that drives kids crazy. You all listen to loud music all day, and you go wild.'

'I do not go wild,' said Jody indignantly.

'And her friends don't go wild, either,' interjected Robie.

'Well, don't get on your high horse,' said Mr Mitford. 'Why don't you hand over the cheque to me, and we'll see if we can rush your job through.'

Jody reached into her purse, her hand automatically groping for her wallet. It wasn't there! She looked down into her purse. 'My wallet!' she exclaimed. She rushed back to her bicycle. Maybe it had fallen out when she had taken her purse off. She remembered doing that as soon as they had arrived at the printer's. She looked all around, but it wasn't there.

Mr Mitford came over and looked at Jody sceptically, as if he didn't believe she had ever had the money. 'I don't know what could have happened to it,' said Jody.

'Are you sure you had it with you?' asked Robie.

'Positive,' said Jody. Robie retraced every step they had taken since arriving at the printer's, but she couldn't find Jody's wallet.

'Well,' said Mr Mitford, 'like we were saying, in these times anything can happen. Only you seem to be running into an awful lot of bad luck lately.' He sounded smug, as if somehow Jody and all young people deserved all the bad luck they could get.

Jody just couldn't believe her wallet was missing.

'I bet somebody stole your wallet at school,' said Mr Mitford. 'I've been reading about crimes in the schools. Kids get their wallets stolen every day. Teachers get beaten up. Schools are a jungle today.'

'They are not,' said Jody, almost in tears. 'Our school is not a jungle.'

'You were lucky nothing worse happened,' said Mr Mitford, gloomily.

'What could be worse?' exclaimed Jody. 'The blank cheque is missing.'

'You'd better stop payment,' said Mr Mitford.

Jody grabbed her bicycle. Mr Mitford was right. She had to get in touch with Michael right away.

'What fool would give you a blank cheque, anyhow?' shouted Mr Mitford as Jody started to leave.

'I wasn't sure how much it would be,' said Jody. 'Besides, it's none of your business.'

'Well, I'm about to close,' said Mr Mitford. 'It's Friday. You'll have to bring another cheque around on Monday.'

'But we need the posters right away,' said Jody. 'Won't you stay open another couple of hours so we can see if we can get a cheque to you?'

'No,' said Mr Mitford with finality. 'I can't do that.' He seemed to soften a little at the sight of Robie's and Jody's distressed faces. 'Well, I'll tell you what. You bring that cheque around Monday before five P.M., and I'll make it a rush job.' He paused. 'But it'll cost you. I can't tell you exactly how much until I check how much work I'll have to put aside to re-do your posters.'

'Thanks,' said Jody.

'Thanks for nothing,' muttered Robie as they rode out of the printer's driveway. 'He acts like it's such a big favour to take our money.'

'I know,' said Jody. 'And I feel like such an idiot for losing Michael's blank cheque. I told him he shouldn't have left it blank.'

'Are you sure you didn't leave your wallet at school?' asked Robie. 'Or at home?'

'No . . . I was careful of it all day because I knew I had the cheque. I know I had it in school. I remember that as I was leaving school, Jake came up and needed to borrow a quarter. I can remember putting my wallet back into my purse, and the cheque was there then.'

Jody and Robie rode by the spot where they had stopped for the fake body in the ditch. They looked all over the ground, but Jody's wallet wasn't there.

Suddenly Jody remembered the sound of the car starting up when she and Robie were in the ditch. She was sure then that someone had deliberately stolen her wallet while she and Robie were in the ditch, and whoever it was had driven off. Jody shivered. It was getting dark. Jody didn't like the thought of someone faking a body in a ditch just to steal a wallet. Perhaps Mr Mitford's gloomy outlook on life was right.

'Let's get out of here,' said Jody. 'I have to call Michael Harper and tell him I lost the cheque. You may get to meet him today, after all.'

'I can think of better circumstances,' said Robie.

5

ONE STRANGE THING

Jody and Robie pulled their bikes over next to a telephone booth. Jody dialled Michael's number. 'You've memorised it already?' asked Robie.

Jody blushed. She wished she didn't blush so easily. She didn't think blushing went with her personality. 'You know I've got a good memory for numbers,' she said. Maths was Jody's best subject.

'I know,' said Robie. 'But this is ridiculous. You dialled his number only once.'

'It's the only rock star's number I know,' said Jody.

The phone rang several times, and no one answered. Jody called her home. Jake answered the phone. Jody told him how her wallet had been stolen.

'That's a mighty peculiar way to stage a robbery,' said Jake. 'It gives me the creeps.'

'It *was* very creepy,' said Jody. 'Anyhow, we'll report it to the police later, but first I've got to get in touch with Michael. I wish I had never let him give me that blank cheque. He hasn't called, has he?'

'No . . . no rock stars, washed up or otherwise, have called since I've been home,' said Jake. 'I know, of course, you think he found you irresistible.'

'Jake, shut up,' said Jody. 'I'm not in the mood to be teased. I've got to get in touch with Michael. Maybe I can reach him at his manager's. I wrote his number on the front of the folder on my desk where I keep things about the concert. Can you get it for me?'

'Yes, ma'am,' replied Jake. 'Hold on . . . Here it is: 742–3982.'

'This concert is turning into a series of disasters,' said Jody. 'It'll be a miracle if it comes off all right.'

'Well, you're good at pulling miracles out of a hat,' said Jake.

Jody smiled. 'I needed that vote of confidence. Thanks. I'll be home soon.'

Jody turned to Robie. 'I've got to call his manager, but I'm out of money. Do you have a dime?'

Robie fished into her jeans and came up with a quarter. 'That's all the change I have.'

'I hate to waste fifteen cents,' said Jody. 'But we don't have much choice.' She dialled the number.

'Hello,' said a pleasantly deep voice.

'Is Michael Harper there?' Jody asked.

'No, he's not.'

Jody hesitated. 'Is this Bud Appleton, his manager?'

'Yes it is. Who is this?'

'It's Jody Markson. I've had something very embarrassing happen.'

Bud Appleton laughed. 'You're the girl who started all this with a letter, aren't you? What's the problem?'

Jody took a deep breath. It was nice of him to skip over the embarrassment and get right to the problem. He sounded like a competent person used to handling problems.

'Well, I don't know if Michael told you that he gave me a cheque for reprinting the posters . . .'

'Yes, he told me about it last night,' said Bud Appleton. 'Look, don't be embarrassed about the posters getting wrecked. What was it, red paint or something? I've never known a concert to go on without a slew of problems. It goes with the territory.'

That's very reassuring, thought Jody, but he doesn't know yet about the lost cheque. 'You don't understand; there's a new problem.' Jody wished she didn't have to go on. She felt like an idiot.

'What's that?' asked Bud, matter-of-factly.

'My wallet was stolen,' said Jody. 'The cheque was in it. I'm so terribly sorry, but I wanted to get in touch with Michael right away. He gave me a blank cheque. I'm so embarrassed.'

Bud laughed easily. 'Luckily, I have the number of the cheque. Michael's an idiot about money. If I let him loose, he wouldn't have a penny left.'

Jody frowned. Bud Appleton and Michael Harper both seemed terribly casual about money. Maybe it came from having so much, but it made Jody uncomfortable. Jody helped her mother keep the family accounts. Mrs Markson was a great lawyer, but she was not good at keeping records. Jody liked to keep the Marksons' records perfectly straight. She knew her mother would never give out a blank cheque, yet Bud Appleton seemed to take it in his stride. He seemed almost too easy-going to believe.

'You poor kid,' said Bud. 'You must feel like you're jinxed.'

'Exactly,' said Jody.

'Well, look, I'll just call the bank. It'll be fine. Are you all right? You and your friend weren't mugged, were you?'

'No,' answered Jody. 'Thanks. It's nice of you to ask, but we're okay. It was the most bizarre way to steal a wallet, though, that I've ever heard of.'

'Yeah, well, there are lots of weirdos running around.'

'This one took the cake,' said Jody. 'And I never saw his face, or hers. It could have been a woman.'

'That's right,' said Bud. 'There are a lot more women bank robbers around than there used to be.'

Robie stood by the phone impatiently. It seemed as if Jody was going to gab to Michael's manager forever.

'Well, look,' said Bud, 'I'd better call my bank right away. I'm really sorry about this.'

'It's after three,' said Jody. 'Will you be able to get in touch with your bank?'

'Don't worry about it,' said Bud. 'They have a twenty-four-hour number I can call. Is there anything else I can do to help?'

'Well,' said Jody, 'I hate to have to keep asking, but if you can cancel the cheque and be sure you don't lose money, we still need money to pay the printer.'

Bud hesitated. It was the first time in the conversation that he seemed not to know exactly what to say.

'We don't need it until Monday,' said Jody quickly. 'The printer will be closed until then.'

'Oh, then that will be okay,' said Bud. He sounded relieved. 'I'll tell you what. I'll stop by and give you another cheque, okay?'

'You will?' said Jody, her voice rising. Bud Appleton sounded so efficient and calm, she had a feeling that maybe the concert would work out, after all.

'Sure. I'll drop by tomorrow afternoon – around three in the afternoon, if that's all right with you.'

'That would be wonderful,' said Jody. She said good-bye and hung up the receiver in a better mood than she had been in all day.

'He wasn't upset about the cheque,' she said to Robie.

'You sure talked long enough.'

'He's very nice,' said Jody. 'He didn't make me feel that it was at all my fault.'

'Well, it wasn't.'

'I know,' said Jody. 'But he could easily have blamed me.' Jody looked thoughtful. 'There was one strange thing, though.'

'You always look for strange things,' said Robie, starting

to get back on her bike. 'What was strange?'

'He mentioned red paint on the posters. He said Michael told him about the red paint, but I didn't tell Michael the paint was red – at least I don't think I did.'

'Stop looking for mysteries. This is a rock concert, not a mystery,' said Robie.

'You're right,' said Jody. 'And, besides, we're going to get our money. He's bringing me the cheque tomorrow. Do you want to come over and meet him?'

'Great,' said Robie. 'I get to meet the manager, and you get to meet the rock star. Thanks, but, no, thanks. Besides, I've got a track meet tomorrow.'

'Hey, Robie,' said Jody, 'I'm really glad you came today. It would have been double creepy without you. I would have hated to find that body alone.'

'Just let me in for some of the good stuff, okay?' said Robie.

Jody grinned, then rode home.

6

WANT TO BET?

Bud Appleton arrived at the Marksons' promptly at three P.M. on Saturday. For once, Jody was eager to answer the door. Appleton was a tall, blond, good-looking man with large brown eyes and a moustache a darker colour than his hair. He smiled at Jody.

'You must be Jody Markson. Had any disasters yet today?'

Jody laughed uneasily. 'No. So far, everything's under control. Will you come in?'

Jake was lying on the living room floor doing some homework. Jake claimed that he could do his homework only when he was in a prone position either on the floor or on a bed. He said that sitting at a desk gave him a headache. Jody introduced Bud to Jake. Jake shook hands, but he seemed to eye Bud coolly.

Bud sat down on the living room couch and looked very relaxed. 'I understand you have a lot of plans for the concert.'

'Yes,' said Jody. 'I thought maybe since Michael wrote "The Joke's on Me" while he was in high school, perhaps we could play up Michael's high school days.'

'That could be a bit awkward,' said Bud. 'How are you going to avoid the subject of the fire?'

'Well . . . obviously we can't, said Jody, 'so I thought we

could confront the issue of the fire out front. After all, Michael was never accused of starting it.'

'No,' said Bud. 'Nothing was ever proved about anybody. Tommy ran away, but . . .'

Jody interrupted excitedly.

'I thought since Michael is coming back to help rebuild the stadium, we could mention the way the stadium burned down and nobody would get upset. It was two years ago, after all. And it's sort of nice that Michael's coming back to help us rebuild it.'

'Hmm,' said Bud. 'It's not a bad idea. It's got some great possibilities for publicity.'

'Do you think Michael will let us do it?' asked Jody eagerly.

'I don't know. He's unpredictable,' said Bud.

'So I noticed,' said Jody. Jake looked up from his book.

'Oh, that's right,' said Bud. 'Let me give you that cheque now, before I forget. You're not giving it to the printer until Monday, is that right?'

'Yes. I'll take it to him right after school on Monday.'

'I made it out for five hundred dollars. Is that enough?'

Jody's eyes lit up. 'It's more than enough,' she said. 'I'm sure it won't be that much. We'll give you the change.'

'Keep it,' said Bud. 'Consider it a donation.'

'Thanks,' said Jody. 'That's very generous.'

Harpo came over and began to sniff at Bud's feet curiously. He wagged his tail.

'He's a nice dog,' said Bud. 'He must be a Bedlington terrier.'

'He's a mutt,' said Jody affectionately, scratching Harpo behind the ear.

'You're wrong. I'm pretty sure he's a Bedlington.'

'No,' said Jody casually. 'Bedlingtons have longer noses and shorter ears. He couldn't be a Bedlington.'

'I wouldn't bet with Jody about dogs or any other animals,' warned Jake.

'I'll bet you a dollar he's a Bedlington.'

Jody looked confused. 'It's a silly bet. It would be hard to prove. We'd have to take him to the vet's, but I'm telling you he's not a Bedlington. He's my dog, after all.'

Bud shrugged his shoulders and smiled. 'Okay, if you don't want to bet.' He glanced around the room, his eye falling on Chico and Harpo, who were tumbling over each other.

'I see you have cats, too. Man's oldest domesticated animal.'

'Not "man's". "People's" oldest domesticated animal,' corrected Jake. With both a mother and a sister who were feminists, Jake was very careful about using sexist language.

Bud smiled again. 'My mistake.' He met Jody's eyes. 'I hope I didn't insult you.'

'No,' said Jody. 'But you made two mistakes. Cats weren't domesticated until in Egypt, around 4,000 B.C. Dogs were used by hunting tribes probably as early as 25,000 B.C. So in comparison with dogs, cats are a new pet.'

'I bet you five dollars you're wrong,' said Bud pleasantly.

'Not five dollars. I can't bet that much, even though I know I'm right,' said Jody. 'But I'll bet you a dollar.'

'You're on,' said Bud. Jody went to the bookshelf and pulled out the encyclopedia and *Man Meets Dog* by Konrad Lorenz. She showed Bud the pages that proved she was right.

Bud smiled a little sheepishly. 'I guess I lost that bet.'

'I warned you,' said Jake. Bud dug into his pocket and took out his wallet.

'Here's a dollar,' he said. 'You can put it in your wallet next to the cheque.'

'New wallet,' said Jody. 'Luckily, Mom had an extra one in the house that she gave to me. I'm going to be sure I don't lose this one.'

Bud looked very concerned for a second, almost troubled.

'Is anything wrong?' Jody asked.

'No . . . no . . . it's just that you're such a nice kid, and you've obviously worked so hard on this concert. I hope it goes well. I just hope Michael's up for this concert. He's been very uptight lately. Personally, I like the idea of the pageant, but . . .'

'But what?' asked Jody.

'Nothing,' said Bud. 'Look, you've got enough to worry about setting up his concert. Michael is my problem. That's what a manager is for.'

The doorbell rang. Jody looked down at Jake, who continued to lie stretched out on the floor. 'Jake,' said Jody sweetly, 'I'm having a meeting.'

'You're closer to the door,' answered Jake.

'I got the door last time.'

Bud looked from one to the other, as if they were slightly crazy. The doorbell rang again.

Jake looked down at his book. 'I bet it's Robie or someone else from your committee,' said Jake.

'You should train your dog to answer the door. After all, he's been domesticated longest,' said Bud.

'Now, that's a good idea, said Jake.

'Do you two go through this every time the doorbell rings?' asked Bud.

'Yes,' said Jake. 'Okay, I'll get it.' Jake hoisted himself off the floor and went to the door.

'See!' Jody and Bud heard Jake yell. 'It was for you, after all.' Michael walked into the living room followed by Jake. If anything, Jody thought the circles under his eyes looked even deeper than the day before.

Bud looked shocked to see him. 'Michael, what are you doing here?'

'I saw your car parked out in front,' said Michael. 'I knew there couldn't be two fire-engine-red Jaguars in town.'

'Is that your Jaguar out front?' Jake asked, hoping to break the tension. 'It's a beauty.'

'Yes,' said Bud. 'It's my pride and joy. If you want, I'll give you a ride in it sometime.'

'That would be terrific.'

'What are you doing over here?' Michael demanded of Bud. 'And why did you leave me that nasty note about giving Jody a cheque? It's my money. I should be able to write a cheque if I want to.'

'Yes,' said Bud. 'But you shouldn't go around giving people *blank* cheques.'

'He's right,' said Jody.

Bud looked at her gratefully. 'See, even a teenager has got more money sense than you do.' Jody looked down at her feet. Technically, Bud was still a teenager himself. He and Michael were only nineteen.

Michael tugged at his forelock nervously. 'What has he been telling you?' he asked Jody.

Jody gave Michael a bewildered look. 'Nothing. He just . . .'

'I'm your manager, Michael, remember,' said Bud smoothly. 'I was just going over some of the details of the concert with Jody, and I gave her a cheque to cover the cost of reprinting the posters.'

'It does more than that,' said Jody.

Michael ignored Jody. 'What details were you discussing?' he asked Bud.

'Hey, Michael, keep cool,' said Bud, getting up and putting his arm around Michael. 'Come on, we can leave together. We've got some stuff to talk over.'

Michael shook Bud's arm off his shoulder. 'Don't tell me to keep cool,' he mumbled. Bud glanced back at Jody and Jake as if to apologise for Michael's behaviour.

'Come on, Michael,' said Bud, 'let's go.'

'And I want to know what you were doing here,' demanded Michael.

'Honestly, Michael,' interrupted Jody, 'he only gave me this cheque, and then we were just talking. We made some silly bets.'

'Not so silly,' volunteered Jake. 'You won a dollar.'

'That's typical,' said Michael. He seemed to take a deep breath and almost collapse. 'All right, Bud,' he said. 'Let's have that talk.' He followed Bud out the door.

Jake watched them go. 'They're quite a duo,' he said. 'They don't seem to like each other very much.'

'I know,' said Jody.

'I hate to say it,' said Jake, 'but if you get out of this concert in one piece, I think you're going to be lucky.'

'What exactly does that mean?' demanded Jody.

'I didn't mean it literally,' said Jake. 'I just think you might have bitten off a little more than you can chew. But you're used to that.'

Jody screwed up her face and gave him a worried look. 'What do you think the odds are that the concert will be a success?'

'I wouldn't want to bet on it,' said Jake.

'Maybe I should make a bet with Bud,' said Jody, half-seriously.

7

A JOKE FROM THE PAST

The next day Jody was alone in the house. Her mother was having Sunday brunch with a friend. Jake was out running. She paced the floor impatiently. She felt anxious and worried.

Jody walked over to her desk. She looked at her checklist of things to do for the concert:

- work out details of pageant
- order programmes
- notify the press
- talk to radio and TV stations about publicity
- put posters up all over town

Order programmes, Jody thought to herself. She had wanted to talk to Michael about the songs he planned to sing. She hoped he would sing some of his songs that were even older than 'The Joke's on Me' – songs that he and Tommy Montag had sung back in high school before Michael became famous.

Jody sighed. Michael had been so tensed up she hadn't talked to him about anything on her checklist. Maybe he was on drugs, she thought. That would explain his nervousness.

Jake often teased Jody that she was too strait-laced. Jody

hated drugs. She had such a logical mind that she couldn't stand it when her friends took drugs and giggled. Jody always wanted things to 'make sense', and she had little patience with people, even her friends, when they didn't care about 'sense'. As far as Jody was concerned, drugs could disappear off the face of the earth, and she wouldn't miss them.

But Michael was a part of the rock music world, and Jody knew that drugs were as available to him as spaghetti, probably easier to get. Jody laughed to herself. When she had been little she had told Jake that spaghetti grew on trees. She had even drawn a spaghetti tree for him. He had believed her until he got to the second grade, and he told his teacher. Jake got furious when he found out that Jody had been teasing him all those years.

Jody turned her mind back to the concert. She was so worried that it was going to be a flop. Drugs answered many of the questions that Jody had about Michael. It would explain why Michael was writing so poorly. Even though Jake argued that many great songs had been written by people on drugs. Jody was convinced that it wasn't true. Jody thought drugs made people stupid, and she had to admit the songs Michael had been writing lately were just that – stupid.

She walked over to the record player and put on Michael's latest record. She had bought it a week ago. The record store had ordered it specially for her. 'Nobody asks for him anymore,' said the record store owner. 'It's strange – a couple of years ago, we couldn't keep Michael Harper's records in stock.'

'He's going to give a concert right here soon,' Jody told the owner. 'Maybe you'll want to stock up on his records.'

The record store owner shook his head no. 'I don't want to get stuck with them,' he said. 'It's a pity. His first record sold like the Beatles. I knew him before he became famous. He and his friends used to come in here all the time.'

'What was he like?' Jody asked.

'Good looking. He used to look like a cherub. Not punk-looking like some of the kids today. He and that boy Tommy Montag used to spend hours in here. And that little Buddy Appleton used to hang out with them.'

'What was Tommy Montag like?' Jody asked.

'He was a tough-looking kid,' said the store owner. 'He looked like the kind of kid who would steal from you if you didn't watch him.'

'Did you ever catch him stealing?' Jody asked.

'No, I guess not. But he looked like he wanted to steal. He and Michael used to argue about what records to buy. Sometimes I would have to kick them out of the store because they'd get so loud.'

'That's interesting,' said Jody. 'They must have had different tastes.'

'Weird tastes if you ask me,' said the owner. 'And a weird sense of humour. I'll never forget the day I found them switching all my records around. They put all the records in different covers, so people buying Beethoven's Fifth went home with The Rolling Stones. It was their idea of a joke. It cost me nearly a whole week's business just to try to sort out my records . . . not to mention all the aggravated customers on my hands.'

Jody had paid for the record and brought it home. Now she thought about that conversation. There were getting to be too many practical jokes connected to this concert – jokes from the past, and disturbing jokes in the present. Jody worried about future jokes.

She went to the record player and put on Michael's new record. It had a bouncy beat, but it sounded childish. The songs sounded like they belonged on 'Sesame Street'. Jake called it 'bubble gum' music, and it sounded like music to chew bubble gum to. 'The Joke's on Me' had a terrific edge to it. These new songs sounded like they had been written by a not very talented seven-year-old:

Have a nice day
Is what you say
But I say, hey!
Hey! Hey! Hey!

It wasn't just stupid. It made no sense. The cheerful little tune sounded like a cheap copy of a TV jingle. 'Oh, well,' Jody mused aloud, flipping the record over. 'Maybe it'll become a collector's item.'

As she lifted the record to change it, Jody glanced at the list of songs on the label in the centre of the record:

'Have a Nice Day' [Harper/Appleton]
'Mary-Go-Round' [Harper/Appleton]
'I Brake for Animals, But You Broke
My Heart' [Harper/Appleton]

'Appleton!' said Jody out loud. 'I didn't realise Michael wrote songs with Bud. I thought he wrote all his songs himself.'

She went to the record cabinet and took out 'The Joke's on Me'. Sure enough, there was only one name – Michael Harper. He had written his best song by himself. Jody couldn't figure out why he was now writing terrible songs with his manager.

Just then, Jake walked into the house. He was sweating from his run. He began to do his cooling-down exercises. 'What's that music?' he asked. He cocked his head toward the record player. '"I Brake for Animals, But You Broke My Heart"?' Jake looked incredulous. 'Am I hearing right?'

'It's on Michael's new album,' answered Jody. 'It's a take-off on Country and Western. I think it's supposed to be a joke.'

'It's not very funny,' said Jake.

'Did you know that Michael's been writing his songs with Bud?' asked Jody.

'No wonder they're so dumb,' said Jake.

'That's mean,' answered Jody. 'What do you have against Bud?'

'I don't like the name "Bud",' said Jake cantankerously.

'His name isn't his fault,' said Jody.

'It's a nickname. It belongs to an eight-year-old.'

'You can't dislike someone just because of his or her name,' insisted Jody.

'It wasn't just his name,' protested Jake. 'He just seemed too cool. I didn't like his moustache, either. Do you think maybe he dyes his hair? His hair was a different colour than his moustache.'

'Even if he does dye his hair, he was very nice. He gave us that big cheque.'

'Bud looks like the kind of person who would write a song called "Have a Nice Day",' said Jake.

'Well, I liked him,' said Jody. 'He seemed sane compared to Michael.'

'That's not much of a comparison,' answered Jake. 'Actually, for all of Michael's craziness, I liked him. Bud strikes me as a phony.'

The phone rang. Jody and Jake simultaneously jumped up, shouting, 'I'll get it!' No one could figure out why the Marksons all liked to answer the phone, but hated to answer the door. Jody and Jake reached the phone at the same time, but Jake was a fraction of a second faster.

'Oh, hi,' he said. Jody stood by his side, impatiently shifting her weight from one foot to the other. Jake mumbled monosyllables into the phone. Deciding that it was one of Jake's friends, Jody walked back to the couch. She had just sat down when Jake held out the receiver. 'It's for you,' he said, deadpan. 'Michael Harper.'

Jody jumped off the couch as if it were wired with electricity. 'Why didn't you tell me?' she whispered. Jake just shrugged his shoulders. Jody grabbed the phone.

'Hi,' she said, sounding to Jake's ears much shyer than she usually did.

'Is that you?' Michael asked. 'You sound different than you did before.'

'It's me,' said Jody. She instantly felt like an idiot. She wished Jake would go into the other room.

'Is that my record playing in the background?' Michael asked.

'Yes,' said Jody. 'I was just listening to it.'

'It's awful,' said Michael vehemently.

'It's not that bad,' said Jody.

'Turn it off!' demanded Michael. 'I can't stand listening to it!'

'Michael . . .' started Jody, but then she realised she didn't know what to say. Perhaps all musicians felt that way about their work, hating to listen to it because they knew the final product wasn't as good as they could make it. However, in Michael's case, it was different. The final product really was quite awful.

'Turn it off, Jody, please!' insisted Michael. Jody put her hand over the receiver. 'Jake,' she said, 'will you turn off the record?'

'Gladly,' said Jake, and Jody was happy she had kept her hand over the receiver.

Michael breathed a sigh of relief when he heard his music go off. 'Thanks,' he said. 'I can't listen to myself. Sorry if I yelled.'

'That's okay,' said Jody.

'Bud just told me about how the first cheque got stolen. But I think he got his story mixed up. Tell me exactly what happened.'

Jody explained about the fake body by the side of the road. 'I think some teenagers must have been waiting for someone to stop.'

'But you didn't actually see anybody?' asked Michael.

'No,' said Jody. 'I didn't even notice my wallet was gone until we got to the printer's.

Michael sighed. 'Has anything else like this happened in

connection with the concert?' Michael asked. 'I mean, besides the paint on the posters and your cheque getting stolen.'

'No,' said Jody. 'Everything was running smoothly. We were able to rent Vickers Stadium. You know about the radio and TV announcements. Everything was fine, unless you count chewing gum on the doorknob.'

'What?' exclaimed Michael. He shouted so loud, Jody had to hold the receiver away from her ear.

'Some kid put chewing gum on my doorknob the other day,' said Jody. 'I got gum all over my hand.'

'Jody,' said Michael. His voice sounded very serious. 'I've got to talk to you. I don't want this concert to backfire on you, and I don't want anyone to get hurt. Can you meet me tomorrow?'

'Sure,' said Jody, 'but I have to go the printer's right after school. Do you want to meet me later?'

'No . . . that'll look . . .' Michael's voice trailed off, as if he were thinking. 'Let me meet you at the stadium before you go to the printer's. We can make it look like we're checking it out for the concert. Then I'll drive to the printer's with you.'

'Why all this mystery?' Jody asked.

'Wait a minute,' said Michael. He seemed to put his hand over the receiver. 'Oh, Bud,' Jody heard him say, 'I didn't realise you were back.' There was a pause.

'Michael?' said Jody. He seemed to forget she was there.

'Oh, yeah,' said Michael. 'Thanks for calling.' He hung up. Jody heard the dial tone. She looked at the phone, bewildered. Michael had called her. She hadn't called him. Why did he want Bud to think that it had been the other way around?

8

MORE JOKES FROM THE PAST

The next morning, riding their bikes to school, Jake looked at Jody. 'Something's up, isn't it?' he asked.

'What are you talking about?' said Jody, sounding annoyed.

'What was that phone call about with Michael?' asked Jake.

'It's nothing that concerns you,' answered Jody. 'There are hundreds of details I've got to take care of for this concert.'

'Don't take that high and mighty tone with me,' said Jake.

'Look, Jake,' said Jody, 'you just don't understand.'

Jake shook his head in disgust. 'Boy, sometimes you can really be snotty, a pill, *and* a jerk. Remember, you're just fourteen months older than I am.'

'Those are fourteen important months,' said Jody.

They rode up to the school just as Robie was locking up her bicycle. Jake locked up his bike and walked away without saying a word.

'What's wrong with him?' asked Robie.

'Oh, nothing,' said Jody. 'I think he just feels left out because he's not running the concert.'

'That doesn't sound like Jake,' said Robie. 'How was your weekend?' Robie asked. 'Did Bud Appleton bring you the cheque?'

'Yes, for five hundred dollars!' Jody grinned. For a second Jody thought about inviting Robie to come to the stadium to meet Michael Harper. *Maybe it would help if another person came with me*, thought Jody. Maybe Michael would relax. She wondered if she was being arrogant, wanting to keep Michael to herself, but she decided to go to the stadium and not tell anyone about it, even Robie, and even Jake.

'Jody!' complained Robie. 'What are you thinking about? You've been staring into space.'

'I'm sorry,' mumbled Jody. 'Come on. We'll be late for class.'

Jody and Robie walked into school together. All day Jody found herself telling half-lies about Michael Harper, and it made her feel very peculiar. She didn't tell anybody about Michael's phone call. Instead, she tried to drum up enthusiasm for the concert, telling everyone how great Michael was and how much he was looking forward to giving the concert.

At one point during the day, as Jody was walking through the hallways, she passed a montage of photos of every graduation class from Shady Brook. This part of the hallway was nicknamed 'The Morgue'. Most of the photos were old and blended in with the dull green paint of the walls. Jody looked at the photo of Michael's senior class. She could pick out Michael with no trouble. Someone had drawn a big star around his face. She looked for Tommy Montag and found his picture. He was standing with his arm loosely draped around Michael's shoulder. It was hard to find traces of the 'punk' described by the record store owner. His hair was long, almost shoulder length, but it looked clean, and he had a wide smile on his face.

'Are you looking forward to seeing your own face up on the wall in a couple of years?' Jody turned around, startled to find Mr MacDonald, her history teacher.

'Oh, no,' said Jody, laughing embarrassedly. 'I was just looking at the photos. I met Michael Harper yesterday.' Jody blushed. She felt like she was bragging.

'That's right,' said Mr MacDonald. 'You're the one who is responsible for his homecoming, aren't you?'

'Well, not exactly,' said Jody. 'But I wrote the letter asking him to help us rebuild the stadium. Did you teach him?'

'Yes, indeed,' said Mr MacDonald. 'Michael Harper and his friends stood out even before he became famous. Michael was a very unusual student, as was his friend Tommy Montag.'

'I was wondering about Tommy Montag,' said Jody.

'He was quite an unforgettable character,' said Mr MacDonald, 'if you know what I mean.'

'No, I don't,' asserted Jody.

'Well,' said Mr MacDonald dryly, 'the first day I had Tommy in my class, he put a "whoopee" cushion on my chair – you know, the kind that make a rude noise when you sit on it. Naturally, the class thought it was a riot. I didn't.'

'I hate practical jokers,' said Jody. 'I've run into an epidemic of them lately.'

'I hate them, too,' agreed Mr MacDonald. 'I had a hard time seeing anything practical about any of Tommy Montag's jokes. Quite the opposite. He glued all the pages of my grade book together once. He was a very popular boy, however, with the other students. He was almost like the Pied Piper. He could get all the other kids, kids who normally were quite good, to go along with his gags. He was quite an unusual boy – and smart, too. Many called him malicious, but I never found him so, though he caused me no end of trouble. None of the jokes he played on me was really malicious.'

'What was Michael Harper like?' Jody asked.

'Now, he had a truly interesting mind,' said Mr MacDonald. 'A little bit weird, as you kids say, but interesting.'

'Weird?' said Jody in shock. It was not at all like Mr MacDonald to use a word like 'weird'.

'Michael Harper loved conspiracies. He did some wonderful research on the John Kennedy assassination, but I couldn't get him to trim down his conclusions to go with the facts. He loved to see conspiracies everywhere. He had one of the most unusual minds I've ever taught. In fact, he and Tommy both were an interesting combination.'

'Did you ever hear them play?'

To her surprise, Mr MacDonald blushed. 'Yes, I used to listen to them often. They were very good, you know.' Mr MacDonald smiled. 'I have to confess that I laughed when "The Joke's on Me" blared out instead of "The Star-Spangled Banner" . . . that was before the stadium burned down, of course.'

'Did most people think it was a good joke?' asked Jody.

'I think so,' said Mr MacDonald. 'Most of us on the faculty were very sorry that Tommy ran away right afterwards. We were prepared to come to his defence. I wonder where he is now. Has anybody heard from him?'

'Not that I know of,' said Jody.

The bell rang for the next class.

'We'd better go,' said Mr MacDonald. 'My class will be coming soon. You mentioned that you had met Michael Harper. Are you seeing him again?'

Jody nodded.

'Please give him my best,' said Mr MacDonald. 'I wonder if he remembers me.'

9

A TRAP

Riding her bike to Vickers Stadium after school, Jody glanced at her watch. She wouldn't have much time. She wanted to be sure she got to the printer's before closing. She was glad that Michael had offered to drive her from the stadium.

The stadium was in a run-down neighbourhood that had almost been urban-renewed out of existence. Few people lived near the stadium anymore. Jody rode by block after block of boarded-up tenements and rubble. The stadium had been built for sports, but now all the professional sports were played in a new stadium out in the suburbs. Vickers Stadium was used only for Shady Brook High Sports, and an occasional rock concert. The school had been able to rent it for a very cheap price, but it was a very depressing place unless full. If only a few hundred people showed up for the concert, the evening would be a disaster.

Jody rode into the empty parking lot and hopped off her bike. She didn't see Michael's pick-up truck. Jake had wondered why he didn't drive a more expensive car, but Jody thought Michael's battered truck was terrific. She hoped he wasn't going to be late.

As she walked across the empty parking lot, Jody felt strange, as if she were on a movie set. She wondered why empty parking lots were so frightening. It was a bright sunny day, and there was nothing intrinsically scary about the asphalt with the white lines, but Jody felt as if threatening music should be playing in the background.

I'm being stupid, Jody thought to herself. *It's probably television's fault. TV always shows shootouts in parking lots. I'm scared for no good reason.* Jody shook her head impatiently. She hated it when she got scared. It made her feel dumb. She ran the last few steps across the parking lot to the stadium box office. It was closed, as she had expected, but she thought the janitor would be nearby. The stadium was only used by the Shady Brook teams when they had an actual big game to play. The teams practised on the fields closer to the school. Jody could see no sign of life. The heavy iron gates to the stadium were shuttered tight.

'Hello!' shouted Jody. 'Is anybody there?' Her voice echoed across the parking lot. Jody tried to peer through the bars of the gates into the stadium. The sunlight filtered in for a few feet, and then there was darkness.

'Hello!' she shouted again. Jody realised she should have called ahead to arrange for her and Michael to go into the stadium. She had merely assumed that a caretaker was always around. She wondered if Michael thought she had keys to the stadium. He might have something to tell her, but he probably would want to check out the stadium, too.

It would be yet another embarrassment if Michael came to look over the stadium and they couldn't get in. Jody decided to see if the janitor was around. She picked her way through the rubble and old newspapers that had blown up against the side of the stadium. As she walked, she checked each of the gates. All were locked. When she got to the far side of the stadium, she thought she heard a noise behind her. She stopped.

'Who's there?' she yelled. Nobody answered. She thought she heard a rustling noise. 'Is anybody there?' she shouted. The rustling noise stopped. Jody hoped it wasn't a rat. She wished she had brought Chico and Groucho along to scare away the rats. She knew that Harpo wouldn't scare away any rats, but she wished she had brought him, also, just for the company.

Jody continued walking around the stadium. When she got to the sixth gate, she heard a creaking noise. The gate was unlocked and swinging slightly in the breeze. It was too heavy to swing freely, but every time it moved just an inch or two it emitted a low creaking noise. Jody put her hand on the metal gate. It felt cold. She realised that this gate alone was completely in the shade.

'Hello!' Jody shouted. Her voice echoed through the stadium. *At least it's got good acoustics*, Jody thought to herself. She debated whether to go into the stadium or to go back to the parking lot to wait for Michael.

I'd better check to see that we can get into the main arena, thought Jody. *Michael will want to have his stage in the centre when he performs*. She took a few steps forward. In the dusk-like light, she could just make out the different stairwells leading to the stands. *I didn't expect it to be so dark inside*, she thought. *I wish I had brought a flashlight*.

Suddenly she heard a creaking sound behind her. *It's that gate*, she told herself silently. *I wish it didn't sound so much like a Halloween sound effect*. She started to walk up the stairs. She wanted to get into the daylight. Her footsteps clanged on the metal stairs. She thought she was hearing the echo of her own footsteps, but suddenly she realised someone else was walking in the stadium. When Jody stopped, the sound of the footsteps continued. Instinctively, Jody climbed faster. She walked through the portals into the stadium and it took her eyes a moment to adjust to the bright sunlight as she looked down at the field. She felt relieved. It had been silly to be frightened. Most likely the footsteps belonged to the janitor, or perhaps to Michael. She opened her mouth to shout 'Hello!' when suddenly her world turned black.

Someone placed a smelly blanket over her head, and

strong arms grabbed her from behind. She tried to yell, but the blanket muffled her cries. She kicked out, and she had the satisfaction of connecting with a leg, but whoever it was only grunted. Jody struggled, but she could feel something soft, like a bunched-up sheet, being wrapped around the blanket effectively pinning Jody's arms to her sides so that she couldn't move. Whoever had attacked her worked quickly and efficiently.

Jody felt herself being picked up and carried down the stairs. She heard a door being opened, and she felt herself being lowered to the ground. Then she heard a door slam shut. She yelled for help, but the part of the blanket that was near her mouth was now all wet from her shouts and it tasted filthy and bitter. Jody knew that no one could hear her shouts. She knew she was all alone, somewhere inside the stadium.

10

SEE JAKE RUN

About the same time Jody was being tied in the blanket, Jake returned home to an empty house. He was still mad at Jody for acting so high and mighty, and he decided to go for a long run. He changed into his running shorts and began his limbering-up exercises. He was lying on his back with his feet over his head in what in yoga is called 'The Plough' position. Jake thought it should be called 'the pretzel'. The doorbell rang.

Harpo barked. *I wish you could answer the door*, thought Jake. *Bud's idea wasn't bad.* Jake muttered to himself as he unrolled and sprang to his feet. He went to the door, and was not overjoyed to see Michael, although Harpo greeted him as if he were a long-lost friend. Jake thought it peculiar that a rock star would be spending so much time with them, even if the whole thing had been Jody's idea. Michael seemed to be trying to peer around Jake to see whether anyone else was in the house.

'Is Jody here?' he asked. 'She was supposed to meet me, but I got a message that she couldn't make it. I was hoping she'd be home.'

'She's not here,' answered Jake coolly. 'I don't know where she is.'

'Are you going running?' asked Michael.

'Yeah,' said Jake noncommittally.

'Do you mind if I take a run with you?' asked Michael. 'I have my running gear in the pick-up, and I need a run.'

'Sure,' said Jake, not quite knowing what else to say.

'Wait a second, while I go get my running gear.'

Michael came back with a very expensive-looking, lightweight bag. It had eight different zippered compartments on the outside and leather straps. There was a picture of a runner in slow motion on the side. Jake carried *his* running gear in an old laundry bag. Michael might drive an old pick-up truck, but he treated himself to the best in running gear.

'You can change in the bathroom,' said Jake. 'I was just doing some warm-up exercises.'

'You can never do enough warm-ups,' said Michael. Jake felt that he was being patronised, and he didn't answer. Michael came out of the bathroom wearing the latest, most lightweight running shorts, and a mesh and nylon running shirt that Jake knew was expensive. Jake wore a faded 'Shady Brook' T-shirt and a pair of gym shorts.

Michael did a few deep-breathing exercises and then he began a series of push-ups. He bobbed up and down with almost frightening ease. The biceps of his arms stood out in bold relief. He was thin, but Jake noticed that he had extraordinarily strong arms for a runner. If Michael took drugs, it certainly wasn't heroin, and it certainly wasn't any drug that sapped his strength.

Michael finished his push-ups and flopped over onto his back. He took a few deep breaths and he had worked up a sweat. 'At least you're human,' said Jake, grudgingly admitting admiration.

Michael grinned. 'People don't realise how much strength you've got to have to sing every night. When I started running, I noticed the difference in my singing right away. It helped tremendously.' Michael did a number of stretching exercises and then he was ready to run.

Jake and Michael walked outside. 'Where do you usually run?' Michael asked.

'I change my route every day,' said Jake. 'I take whatever street has the least traffic, and I wind up in the park.'

'Okay, I'll follow you,' said Michael. They started out, but soon Michael took the lead. Only gradually did Jake realise he was probably running almost a minute a mile faster than he usually did. In truth, Jake was a secret competitor. Because he joked around so much and seemed to be easy-going, few people realised how much he hated to be beaten at anything.

As they turned into the park, Jake could see the sweat pouring off Michael's body, and he could feel great puddles of sweat dripping down his own back. Harpo was running by his side. Ordinarily, Harp looked like he loved Jake's running, but now even Harpo looked as if he were concentrating on keeping up with Michael.

I'm not going to be able to keep this up much longer, Jake thought to himself. *What in the world am I trying to prove to myself, anyway?*

Michael looked back at Jake and smiled. Jake wanted to kill him. Suddenly a thought flashed through Jake's mind. Could Michael deliberately be running at a fast pace because he wanted to tire Jake out?

Jake shook the sweat away from his eyes. *I'm being paranoid*, he thought to himself. *Just because the guy is a rock star, and can run faster than me, I'm jealous. Jody would laugh at me if I told her what I was thinking*. Jake kept running. At least he was no longer mad at Jody, he thought to himself.

11

LOCKED IN THE LOCKER ROOM

Jody was determined not to cry. If only the blanket didn't taste so awful or weren't pulled so tightly over her head. She kept feeling as if she were suffocating. 'You're not suffocating,' she told herself. She spoke out loud. Her voice sounded strange, all muffled up in the blanket, but it made her feel better to hear her own voice.

'I'm going to talk out loud from now on,' she said, as if there were someone in the room listening. Suddenly, she realised there could be someone in the room guarding her, but she didn't think so. The blanket was so thick that she couldn't see anything.

'Either the blanket is thick, or I'm in a dark room,' she said. 'And if someone is here, answer me.' She waited to see if anyone would speak up. Nothing happened. She rolled to her left. Within a few feet, she came to a metal wall. It sounded hollow when she bumped into it. She rolled to her right and hit another metal wall.

'Locker!' shouted Jody. 'I'm locked in a locker room!' She started to giggle, and then within seconds she felt herself wanting to cry. She made herself stop. 'No more jokes,' she swore, but she said it softly, as if she didn't want anyone else to hear her. She could feel panic bubbling up inside her.

'Talk to yourself,' she commanded. 'If you're talking to yourself, you'll stay in control. There's got to be a way out of here.' Jody rolled in each direction of her prison. She was in a small room lined on three sides with lockers. By the process of elimination, she knew which wall had the door, and she kicked at the door with her feet. The thumping noise echoed through the locker room. Jody could only hope that it sounded throughout the stadium. Somebody would come eventually.

Michael would see her bicycle outside the stadium and come to look for her. Suddenly, Jody felt a sinking feeling in the pit of her stomach. Michael was the only one who knew she was coming to the stadium. Could he have been the person who tied her up? Jody felt her heart racing. Why would Michael tie her up? If he wanted to back out of the concert, all he had to do was cancel. This attack didn't make any sense, but then Jody remembered that Michael did not always talk as if he were making sense. If it hadn't been Michael, Jody couldn't imagine who it had been. It conceivably could have just been some rough kids in the neighbourhood who were playing a vicious prank, but Jody felt that somehow the attack had to be connected with the concert.

Despite the blanket, Jody shivered. The only reason for the blanket would be that the assailant didn't want Jody to see his face. *He must have known I'd recognise him*, thought Jody. *It had to be someone I know, and who could it be besides Michael?* She kicked her feet in frustration. The sheet loosened just a little, not enough for her to get free, but enough so that she could stand up.

'I must look like Mr Peanut,' she said aloud to herself. She kept trying to move her arms, but the blanket wouldn't move. 'When I get out of here, I'll probably never sleep with a blanket again,' Jody swore. She explored the locker room, with the blanket over her head, nudging the lockers with her body. Then she lay back down on the floor and stamped her feet against the door again, hoping this time someone would hear her.

She took a deep breath, forcing more of the dust from the blanket into her nose. *'I hate you!'* she screamed to the person who had tied her up. *There*, she thought, *I'm glad I yelled that. I wonder how long it will be until Jake and Mom start to look for me.* Jody fought back despair and hysterics. She knew that if she allowed herself to think that she might not be rescued, she would fall apart. She had to believe that either she would get out through her own efforts, or someone would come and rescue her. She couldn't allow herself to think that whoever had tied her up might come back before she was rescued.

If they had wanted to really hurt me, or kill me, they would have done it right away, Jody thought. *If I am being kidnapped, Mom and Jake will get me out.* Yet deep inside, Jody knew this wasn't an ordinary kidnapping. She had been trussed up like a turkey because someone wanted her out of the way. Something about the way she was being treated reminded her of the cruelty of the person who had stuffed the clothes to look like a body.

Jody knew the two events were related. She promised herself that when she got free, she and Jake would find the connection. They had solved mysteries before. They would solve this one. And this one was personal. Jody wanted to teach the cruel person a lesson. 'Come on, Jake,' she urged aloud. Jake could often sense when Jody was in danger. Jody was a very logical person. She didn't believe in astrology. But right now she believed in E.S.P. with all her heart. She had to believe. It was almost her only hope.

12

SEE JAKE WORRY

Jake wasn't getting any message. The only message his brain was sending was 'Stop running!' He could feel himself lose power in his legs, and he knew he couldn't run much farther. He had long since used up his second wind, his third wind, and each new spurt of energy now seemed used up in seconds. However, Michael was still running easily, a couple of lengths in front.

'Hey, Michael!' Jake finally shouted. 'I've got to slow down. You're too fast for me.'

Michael slowed down. 'I feel terrific. Sometimes it helps to run with someone a little faster than you.'

Jake gave him a dirty look. While what Michael said was true, something about his tone was irritating. Michael sounded too cheery; it was almost a fake cheeriness. He seemed cocky.

'You know, I almost feel as if I could write a song,' said Michael.

'You said before you tried to write songs *out* of your head when you run,' said Jake.

'Well, if you listened to the junk I've been doing lately, you'd know why.' A shadow from a tree fell across Michael's face, and Jake couldn't read his expression but he thought he saw him wince.

'"The Joke's on Me" was a great song, and you wrote that one by yourself. Why did you start writing songs with Bud Appleton?' Jake asked.

'How did you know about that?' Michael asked sharply.

'It's not exactly a secret,' said Jake. 'Jody read it on the label of the record.'

'But nobody usually reads that fine print,' said Michael. He sounded angry.

'You don't know my sister,' said Jake. 'She doesn't miss a thing.'

'I just hope she isn't too curious for her own good,' mumbled Michael. Jake could barely hear him. He realised that Michael had never answered his question about why he collaborated with Bud. He asked it again. 'After all,' added Jake, 'you two don't seem to get along very well.'

'Gilbert and Sullivan hated each other,' said Michael. 'They stopped speaking, but they kept writing songs together. They used to do it through the mail.'

'Yeah, but they wrote great music,' said Jake. As soon as he said it, he wished he could take his words back. Michael looked very hurt. Jake realised that Michael might feel free to put his music down, but he didn't like Jake to do it. Jake had learned that no matter how much his friends told him that their family was awful, it was best never to agree with them and tell them they were right. Jake could tell from Michael's expression that the same applied to a person's songs.

Still, why would Michael collaborate with Bud? Jake couldn't figure out an answer. Michael's music had been one hundred per cent better when he had written his own songs. They had now circled the park twice. Jake figured they had run almost seven miles. He was exhausted, but he didn't want to be the one who said 'Let's stop'. It had been bad enough to be the one who had to ask Michael to slow down. Jake had run ten miles three times in his life. They were now running at a slow enough pace that Jake figured he could keep going for a while.

Outwardly, Jake might not seem as curious as Jody, but when something or, more particularly, *someone* mystified Jake, he always wanted to know more. Jake was puzzled by Michael. It was like being around quicksilver.

'What's it like to work with someone you don't like?' Jake asked.

'Why do you want to know?' asked Michael. They were running so much slower now that Jake was finding it easy to talk.

'I'm just curious about how you two hooked up. Jody and I work together a lot, and though I get mad at her, we get along.'

'You two are really very close for a brother and sister,' commented Michael.

'Well, after my folks got divorced, we kind of took care of each other,' said Jake, wondering how he could get the conversation back to Michael. Michael was very clever at avoiding questions he didn't want to answer.

'How long has Bud been your manager?' Jake asked, deciding to take a different tack.

'Since I started,' said Michael. Every time Jake mentioned Bud, Jake could see Michael tense up.

'Where did you meet him?' Jake asked.

'We grew up together,' said Michael. 'I've known him most of my life.'

'Did he go to Shady Brook?' asked Jake.

'Yeah. He dropped out of high school when we were juniors,' said Michael. 'Then Bud travelled around for a while.' Jake wondered whether 'travelled around' was a euphemism for dealing in drugs. A lot of drug dealers 'travelled around' the country. Jake also wondered whether it was his imagination or whether Michael had in fact started to pick up the pace. Suddenly, Jake felt a sharp pain in his side. He gasped.

'Anything wrong?' Michael asked blandly.

'I've got a stitch,' said Jake. 'It really hurts.' Jake staggered over to the edge of the road. He bent over, his hand pressed to his side.

'Lie down on your back,' said Michael. 'We can rest for a while.' Jake lay down on the grass by the side of the road. Harpo lay down beside him, panting heavily. Harpo seemed extremely grateful for the opportunity to rest. Jake sighed. It felt wonderful to just lie down. His legs felt like overcooked spaghetti.

The grass felt cool and wonderful underneath him. Jake closed his eyes. When he opened them again, the sky had turned deep blue and there were red streaks from the sunset above his head. Harpo was sound asleep beside him. Jake rolled over. He knew he hadn't fallen asleep. He didn't think he had been resting more than five minutes, but he felt unaccountably anxious. He didn't see Michael anywhere.

'Michael!' he yelled.

Michael came out of a bunch of trees in the park. 'I just went for a walk. You seemed to be resting peacefully.'

'I've got to go home,' said Jake.

'Let's just talk,' said Michael. 'I've got a song in my head, and I want to give it a chance to simmer. You gave me the idea.'

'I did?' Jake asked querulously. He felt a blister on his left foot. With the sun nearly set, he felt cold. Tired and chilled, he found it hard to get up much enthusiasm for Michael's song. Michael ignored Jake's bad mood.

'Yeah. You asked me how I got hooked up with Bud, and the words "Hooked on the Past" came to me,' said Michael, sounding excited. 'I've got the start of a tune.'

'Terrific,' said Jake sarcastically. He tried to jog, limping because of his blister.

'Thanks,' said Michael, not hearing the sarcasm. 'I have a good feeling about this song. It's funny, but your sister's idea to get me back home for this concert may turn out to be the best thing that ever happened to me.'

Jake was barely listening. All he could think of was how

great a shower would feel, a hot, hot shower. He and Michael jogged slowly home.

When they got back to the house, Jake was surprised to see Jody's bike wasn't there. Jake suddenly could identify the anxious feeling he had been having. He was anxious about Jody. Jake rushed into the house.

'Is anybody home?' he shouted. His voice echoed through the house.

Jake looked down at his watch. Seven o'clock. Jody should have been home. Jake dialled his mother's office. Mrs Markson picked up the phone herself.

'Hi, Jake,' she said. 'I tried to call you and Jody, but no one was home. I have to work late tonight. I'll be home around nine.'

'Mom, have you talked to Jody this afternoon?' Jake asked.

'No,' said Mrs Markson.

'Michael Harper came by. We just took a run. He says Jody cancelled a meeting with him. Mom, I'm worried.'

Michael gave Jake a strange look.

'Why are you worried?' asked Mrs Markson. 'It's not that late.'

'I've got a feeling,' Jake whispered. He didn't want Michael to hear.

Mrs Markson paused. She had always thought it was strange that Jake had turned out to be the 'worrier' in the family, but she loved him for it, and she respected the unusual bond between her two children. Even as little children, they had always seemed to sense when one or the other was in trouble. They might tease each other and fight, but Mrs Markson knew there was much love between them. Her own instinct would have been not to worry about Jody. It was still early in the evening, and Jody might be anywhere, but if Jake was concerned, Mrs Markson wouldn't take it lightly.

'I'll come home right away,' said Mrs Markson.

'Thanks, Mom,' said Jake, relief sounding in his voice. 'I'll make some phone calls to Jody's friends to see if anyone knows where she is.'

Jake called Robie first. She couldn't help him. Robie said Jody had told her she had a lot of running around to do for the concert, but nothing specific. Every place Jake called, he got the exact same story. Jody had told several people she had many errands to do, but nobody knew exactly where she had planned on going. When he called the printer and discovered she hadn't showed up with the cheque, Jake became truly concerned. Jake was just slamming the phone back onto the receiver after his sixth call when his mother came into the house.

'Nobody has seen her,' he said. 'I tried everybody I could think of.'

Mrs Markson looked perplexed. 'She could have gone for a ride on her bike. It's a beautiful day.'

'No,' insisted Jake. 'She's so involved in this concert she'd never just take an afternoon off – certainly not without going to the printer's. Something's wrong.'

Michael had brought his guitar into the house and was quietly strumming it. 'He makes himself right at home, doesn't he?' whispered Mrs Markson.

Jake scowled. 'Yeah. Don't disturb him. He's on a creative binge. "Hooked on the Past."'

'The only binges I allow in my house are food binges,' said Mrs Markson. 'Michael,' she said, raising her voice, 'would you tell me exactly what Jody said when she called to cancel your meeting?'

'She didn't say anything,' said Michael. His fingers moved down the neck of his guitar. 'She left a message.' Michael changed his chords. His eyebrows furled together and he seemed to be concentrating deeply.

'Who took the message?' asked Mrs Markson impatiently. Jake recognised the tone of voice she often used on hostile witnesses at a trial.

'I don't know. I guess someone at the hotel did.'

'Where were you going to meet her?' asked Jake urgently. He couldn't imagine why he hadn't asked Michael earlier. Jake decided that all that running had addled his brain.

'At Vickers Stadium,' answered Michael. 'I wanted to check it out, and I wanted a place to talk to her without anyone interrupting.' Michael turned back to his guitar and started strumming. Chico and Groucho seemed to be fascinated with the movement of his fingers on the guitar strings. They both looked liked they wanted to pounce.

'I don't know why you're so upset,' said Michael, but he sounded upset and nervous himself. 'She's fifteen. When I was her age, I used to split all the time. Your sister splits for a couple of hours, and you act like the sky is falling.'

Jake ignored him. He turned to his mother. 'I'm going to the stadium,' he said. 'It's the only clue we've got.'

'Clue?' said Michael in a mocking voice. 'The case of the missing sister?'

'Wipe that smirk off your face,' said Jake furiously.

'Hey, Jake,' said Michael, 'I was just kidding. I didn't realise you were really worried. I'll drive you to the stadium if you really want to look for her.' Jake looked at his mother.

'It's a good idea. If he drives you, I can stay here and wait by the phone in case Jody calls.' Harpo leaped to his feet, wagging his tail furiously.

'Okay, boy, we'll take you,' said Jake.

Michael looked at him quizzically.

'He may be able to find Jody faster than we can.'

13

THE RESCUE

Jody was exhausted. She had no idea how long she had been tied up. It had seemed like hours, but she knew that each minute wrapped up in the blanket seemed stretched out. Her arms ached from being pinned to her sides. More than anything she wanted to get that blanket off so she would be able to see again. But even though she struggled and rolled around on the floor, the sheet holding the blanket remained secure. It was all she could do to keep from crying.

She didn't hear the sound of Michael's pick-up when he and Jake drove into the parking lot. Jake saw Jody's bike and shouted, 'There's Jody's bike! There's Jody's bike!' Jake practically jumped out of the pick-up before Michael came to a complete stop.

'Take it easy,' said Michael. He tugged at his hair nervously. He seemed to be stalling. 'We'll find her. Maybe she thought I didn't get her message and she's waiting.'

Jake looked at him sceptically. The sun had set, and the stadium loomed up in the twilight, looking like a monument from ancient times. Harpo ran up to the stadium and began to circle it. Jake followed him, shouting, 'Jody! Jody!' His voice bounced off the stone walls.

Jody did hear Jake's voice. 'I'm here!' she screamed. Jake's voice sounded far away. She hoped he could hear her through the blanket. She thumped her feet against the side of the door.

From where he stood, Jake thought he heard a sound from within the stadium, but he wasn't sure. Harpo found the creaking, open gate at the back of the stadium, the same one Jody had gone through, and dashed inside. Jake couldn't see where he had gone. He shouted for Harpo, but he got no answering bark.

'Wait a second,' said Michael. 'I've got a flashlight in the pick-up. I'll get it.'

There was just enough light for Jake to make out the metal staircases. He couldn't wait for Michael to come back with the flashlight. He yelled out Jody's name. The sound echoed eerily and bounced back to him. He heard a faint answering thump, but he couldn't figure out in what direction it was coming from. Jake stood very still. Then he yelled. Once again he heard a dull thud. No animal would be thumping every time it heard his voice. The thump had to be coming from Jody. Jake wondered why she didn't just shout.

Jake was wrong. Jody was shouting, but the room where she was locked up was below him, and her voice was still muffled by the blanket. Luckily, the sound of her feet pounding on the door did carry. Jody lay on her back and kicked at the door with all her might. Suddenly she heard a bark.

'Harpo!' she cried.

Jake ran down the staircase following the sound of Harpo's bark as best as he could in the dark.

'Why is he barking? Has he found her?' asked Michael in a whisper.

Jake spun around. He had been concentrating so hard that he hadn't heard Michael return with the flashlight. He looked down at Michael's sneakers. *Did Michael have a reason for moving without making any noise?* Jake wondered.

'Jody is in the stadium somewhere,' said Jake. 'Otherwise, Harpo wouldn't be so excited. We have to follow his bark.'

Jake ran down the hallway in the direction of Harpo's bark. Finally, he reached the locker room door. Harpo was scratching at it with his paw, trying to get it open.

'Jody!' yelled Jake. 'Jody! Jody!'

'Help!' answered Jody. This time Jake heard her. He twisted the knob. It was unlocked. He almost fell on Jody, who had been lying on the floor so she could use her feet to knock on the door.

'What the . . . ?' yelled Jake, shocked at the sight of Jody wrapped in the blanket with only her feet sticking out.

'Get me free!' cried Jody. Jake pulled at the sheet, which had been tied tightly around the blanket.

'You look like a bed-roll,' said Jake, finally getting the sheet off.

'Thanks,' mumbled Jody. The sheet fell away and Jody threw the blanket off. Harpo leaped into her lap, licking her face.

Michael beamed the flashlight all around the locker room. 'Are you all right?' he asked. He sounded horrified.

Jody nodded. She looked around her prison, for the first time being able to see it. The room was filled with large old-fashioned lockers, big enough for a person to hide in.

Jake followed the direction of her eyes.

'Was someone hiding in one of the lockers when they jumped you?'

'No,' said Jody. 'I was upstairs when someone threw a blanket over my head and carried me down here.' Jody stood up, leaning on Jake for support.

'Come on,' said Jake. 'We'll get you home and call the police.'

'Wait a minute,' said Jody. 'We have to find my purse.'

'What a time to worry about your purse,' said Michael.

'No, you don't understand,' said Jody. 'My purse had a cheque from Bud Appleton. If it's gone . . .' Jody's voice trailed off.

'I told you, don't worry about that,' said Michael, almost

savagely. 'I'll see that you get your money.' Jake sensed that Jody felt that finding her purse was very important.

'I'll look for it,' he said. 'Wait here.'

'Thanks,' said Jody softly. 'I don't think I could walk in there again. I was attacked at the top of the staircase. Look, there.' Jody shivered.

'Here,' said Michael, 'take the flashlight.' Michael helped Jody up. They walked to the pick-up to wait for Jake. Michael handled her as if she were fragile china.

'Are you sure you weren't hurt?' asked Michael.

'No. I was terrified,' said Jody. 'But I wasn't physically hurt. I don't know why someone did it. Maybe it was a practical joke, or maybe someone is really out to get me. Maybe someone wants me to stop working on the concert.'

At the words 'practical joke', Michael almost jumped out of his skin. 'What did you say about it being a joke?' he asked.

'I said, "practical joke",' repeated Jody deliberately, 'like the kind you and your friend Tommy Montag used to play.'

'I swear,' said Michael desperately, 'I didn't have anything to do with this.'

'But you know something about it, don't you?' said Jody. 'You know who tied me up.'

'No,' said Michael. 'No . . . it's just . . .'

'Just what?' demanded Jody. 'Who has been playing all these horrible jokes on me just because I'm in charge of your concert?'

'I need time,' said Michael, almost to himself. Then he looked at Jody. 'I promise you, I'll explain it all to you when I can.'

Jody looked straight ahead. She didn't know all the answers, but she had plenty of suspicions, and she wasn't going to wait for Michael Harper to decide to give her the answers. She and Jake would discover the answers themselves as to who was trying to scare her away from putting on the concert.

Michael looked extremely uncomfortable, almost scared.

Jake came running out of the stadium. 'No sign of your purse anywhere,' he said, 'I didn't like being in there alone.'

'At least you could move around,' said Jody. 'You weren't tied up.'

14

THE GREATEST PRACTICAL JOKE IN THE WORLD

Mrs Markson looked shocked when she saw Jody. Jody's hair was matted to her face. Her clothes were filthy.

'What happened to you?' asked Mrs Markson anxiously.

'I'm okay, Mom,' said Jody, leaning on her mother. 'It's a long story.'

'I've got to go,' said Michael, staring at Jody. 'I'm so sorry. This won't happen to you again.'

'I won't let it,' warned Jody. She sounded determined. Her mother led her inside to the couch. As soon as Jake told her how he had found Jody, Mrs Markson called the police.

Jody lay on the couch and shivered. Her mother brought her a blanket – a clean blanket – and tucked it around her. Jody had thought she would never want to see a blanket again, but shock had turned to chills, and she couldn't seem to keep warm. The police came and Mrs Markson explained to them what had happened. She brought the policeman and policewoman in to see Jody. Mrs Markson hovered over her daughter, urging her to take sips of warm tea laced with honey.

'I find it so hard to believe she was attacked,' Mrs Markson explained to the police. 'I keep wondering whether it was someone I knew – some crazy client who thought I didn't do a good enough job defending him.'

Both the policeman and policewoman knew Mrs Markson from her many appearances in criminal court. They nodded their heads. 'It could have been someone out to get revenge,' said the policewoman.

'I still don't think it had anything to do with you, Mom,' said Jody. She twisted the edge of her blanket. 'I think someone wanted to get hold of my purse.'

'That was a terribly elaborate purse-snatching,' said Mrs Markson.

'It's a trademark,' said Jody.

'What do you mean?' demanded Mrs Markson.

'It's the second time my purse has been taken, and each time I've been carrying a cheque from either Michael Harper or Bud Appleton. It's too much of a coincidence.'

'You say you had no hint of who attacked you?' asked Mrs Markson. 'Nothing that would help the police?'

'I never saw my attacker,' said Jody. 'All of a sudden I felt the blanket over my head, and the next thing I knew I was being dumped in the locker room.'

'Who knew you were going to the stadium?' asked the policeman.

Jody hesitated. She wanted publicity for the concert, but not this kind. She looked at her mother. 'Can you keep it confidential?' she asked the policeman.

'We'll try,' said the policewoman.

'Michael Harper,' whispered Jody.

To her relief, the name didn't seem to register with the police. Jody wondered whether Michael would be happy or sad that his name hadn't been recognised.

The police seemed impatient. The policewoman closed her notebook. 'We don't have much to go on,' she said. 'We'll make some inquiries around the stadium, but, after all, you weren't hurt.'

'She looked more like Mr Peanut,' volunteered Jake.

The policeman shrugged his shoulders. 'I'm sorry, Mrs Markson, but you know how overworked we are. We'll try to look into it. But I can't make any promises.'

'If you can think of anything else that can help us,' said the policewoman, 'let us know.' She smiled. 'Meanwhile,' added the policewoman, 'keep out of empty stadiums.'

'That's terrific advice,' Jake whispered to Jody.

'Shh!' said Mrs Markson, and she walked the police to the door.

'Somehow, I don't think they are going to give this top priority,' said Jake when she got back.

'I know,' said Mrs Markson, 'but you really can't blame them. In a way, it is just an elaborate purse-snatching. They get ten purse-snatchings a day, at least.' Mrs Markson seemed to shift her focus. 'Do you think Michael Harper engineered the attack? He seems like a strange young man. I should have kept him here for the police to question.'

'I'm glad you didn't,' said Jody. 'We don't need that kind of publicity. Besides, I don't think it was Michael. He seemed shocked when Jake found me.'

'He's an entertainer, remember,' said Jake. 'He could be a wonderful actor. Besides, he might have planned on getting me out of the way this afternoon.'

'What does that mean?' asked Jody sharply.

'Michael came over looking for you. He took me on a long run until I was exhausted. Harpo practically couldn't keep up.'

Jody closed her eyes. 'Are you exhausted, honey?' asked Mrs Markson.

'No, I'm okay. I'm just sleepy, I guess.'

'Why don't you go up to bed?' said Mrs Markson. 'Jake and I will help you up.'

'Mom, I can walk,' said Jody impatiently. 'But I guess I would like to go to bed.' Jody threw the blanket on the floor.

'I'll go up with her,' said Jake quickly, sensing that Jody

wanted to talk to him alone. Up in her room, Jody sank into her bed gratefully.

'It feels so good to be home,' she whispered.

'It was awful, wasn't it?' said Jake.

'Worse than awful,' said Jody. 'I was so scared. I didn't want to tell Mom how terrible it was. Jake, I'm still scared. It's as if I stumbled into quicksand. Everything about this concert seems treacherous, and I don't understand it.'

'Somebody must think that if they can scare you off, the concert will be cancelled. They're probably right. After all, it was your idea. I'm still suspicious of Michael. Something about that run this afternoon didn't make sense. I've got a big ego, but even *I* don't think a nineteen-year-old rock star would want to go running with me. He wanted to keep track of me, or find out something from me, but I can't figure out what. I tried to find out things from him, but all I found out was that Bud Appleton dropped out of Shady Brook.'

'I know,' said Jody. 'He used to hang around with Michael and Tommy Montag.' Jody looked down at her blanket and ran her hand over the silk edge, a habit she had since she was a baby. Chico and Groucho were purring on either side of her.

She glanced up at Jake. 'Can you keep a secret?' she asked.

'That's the dumbest question you ever asked me. The answer is no.'

'I'm being serious,' said Jody.

'I know,' said Jake. 'That's why I'm insulted.'

'Okay,' said Jody. 'I'm sorry I asked you. I guess I do it from habit.' Jody smiled.

'It's a lousy habit,' snapped Jake.

'I said I was sorry.'

Jake laughed. 'I am, too. I guess I'm on edge. It was scary finding you all tied up like a chicken.'

'Scarier to be the one tied up,' said Jody. She paused. She pulled nervously at the edge of her blanket. 'I've been asking questions about what Michael Harper did before he became famous. Guess what I found out?'

'That he liked to play practical jokes,' said Jake. 'I thought maybe these jokes on you might be related to the fire at the stadium.'

'Apparently it was Tommy Montag who was the great prankster,' said Jody. 'Michael pretty much just went along with him. Tommy used to do things like glue the pages of Mr MacDonald's grade book together. He once changed all the records at the record store into the wrong jackets.'

'He sounds like great fun,' said Jake sarcastically.

'Tommy Montag disappeared right after the stadium burned down,' said Jody. 'Nobody ever saw him again. For a while, people were afraid he had been killed in the fire, but they found no traces of a body. So everyone assumed he ran away. He's never been seen since.'

'Did they ever prove that he started the fire?'

'No,' said Jody, 'but everyone assumed he did. Michael was questioned, but he swore that he didn't have anything to do with switching the wiring. Michael even offered to take a lie-detector test at the time of the fire.'

'All that was two years ago,' said Jake. 'Why is someone so upset about the idea of Michael Harper giving the benefit to rebuild the stadium?'

Jody didn't answer his question. Instead, she toyed with her blanket. Finally, she asked, 'What would be the greatest practical joke in the world?'

'I don't know,' said Jake. 'Short-sheeting the President's bed?'

Jody shook her head.

'How about being an invisible joker?' she said. 'Everyone thinks you've disappeared. You come back. You and your best friend can plan lots of jokes and nobody thinks of blaming you, Michael and Tommy could be working together, or maybe Tommy's working alone.'

'Wait a minute,' said Jake. 'Why would they keep picking on you?'

'That's one of the things we have to find out. There are a

number of holes in my theory. I've made a list.'

Jake groaned. Jody was always making lists.

Jody ignored Jake. She got out a piece of paper from under the covers. She handed it to Jake.

1. How did he find out I was in charge of the concert?
2. How did he know I would be going to the printer in order to play the trick with the fake body?
3. How did he know I was going to the stadium?
*4. Why is he so intent on stealing the cheques?

'Why is number 4 starred?' Jake asked.

'Because somehow it's the question I least understand. For the others, I could think of a plausible explanation, but number 4 has me stumped,' said Jody.

'So what do we do now?' asked Jake. 'Confront Michael Harper with your theory? He could have told Tommy you were going to the stadium. You're right. They could have planned the attack on you together.'

'I don't think we should confront Michael with our theory yet,' said Jody. 'He could deny it. I had the feeling from what he said to me while we were waiting for you at the stadium that he wants to confront Tommy Montag himself. No, I think we've got to do more looking into Tommy Montag's background. I'm convinced that he's the key. We can pretend we're doing research for our pageant for the concert.'

'All right,' said Jake. 'But no more going off on your own. If Tommy Montag is the invisible jokester, I don't like his sense of humour.'

'Don't worry,' said Jody, 'neither do I. I have no intention of living through anything like this afternoon ever again.'

15

LITTLE JOKES

The next morning Jody woke up feeling fine. She was surprised how easily the effects of being tied up seemed to have disappeared. Groucho and Chico slept at the foot of her bed. Groucho sensed she was awake and stealthily moved his way up and sat down right next to her face, purring steadily.

'Good morning,' said Jody, and she petted him lazily.

She heard a knock on her door.

'Who is it?' she yelled.

'Jake.' He peeped his head in the doorway. 'How are you?'

'I feel fine,' said Jody. 'I didn't even have nightmares.'

'You don't have to sound like Wonder Woman,' said Jake. 'I dreamed about being locked up in a closet.'

Jody laughed. 'We've got a lot to do today.'

'Unravelling the mystery of who is trying to bust up your concert?'

'Exactly,' said Jody. 'That reminds me. I've got to call Bud Appleton. Hand me the phone.'

The phone rang five times before anyone answered. Bud sounded as if he were asleep. 'Hello,' he grunted.

'It's Jody Markson. Did I wake you up?'

'Yes,' groaned Bud.

'I'm so sorry,' said Jody. Jake watched her blush.

'It's all right. I'm glad you're okay. Michael told me about the horrible thing that happened to you at the stadium.'

'It was a nightmare,' said Jody. 'The worst thing is that they stole your cheque.'

Bud laughed uneasily. 'That cheque is bouncing around as if it were made out of rubber.'

'It's not funny,' insisted Jody. 'I'm convinced someone is trying to stop me from putting on this concert.'

'Well, you have to admit,' said Bud, 'the concert was your idea, and you are in charge of most of the details.'

'Whoever is trying to stop me is not going to succeed,' said Jody.

'I wouldn't want to bet against you,' said Bud. He sounded thoughtful. 'Why don't you stop by my hotel at five this afternoon and I'll give you another cheque?'

'Could it be earlier?' Jody asked. She felt embarrassed, but she needed to get the money to the printer as soon as possible.

'No,' said Bud crossly. Jody didn't want to push him. It was bad enough that she had woken him up.

'All right,' said Jody. She hung up the phone. 'We're meeting him at five,' she told Jake. 'I've got to call the printer.'

Although the printer was disgruntled, he agreed to stay at his shop until six-thirty to give Jody time to bring over the cheque.

'That'll be great,' said Jody after hanging up the phone. 'That will give us time to visit Tommy Montag's mother after school.'

'Why are we seeing her?' asked Jake.

'We have to start somewhere,' said Jody. 'And who else would know more about Tommy?'

During her lunch break at school, Jody called Mrs Montag and arranged to visit her at three-thirty. Jody and Jake rode their bikes to her house as soon as classes were over. Mrs Montag turned out to be a pleasant-looking plump woman who seemed to smile a lot. Her smile seemed more like a nervous tic than any indication of friendship or pleasure, and it spread over her face at odd moments. She invited Jody and Jake into her house and offered them a soft drink. Jake inspected his glass, half-expecting it to be a 'dribble glass', a fake glass sold in novelty shops that would make him slobber his drink all over his chin.

'I'm in charge of a concert Michael Harper is giving to rebuild the stadium,' explained Jody. 'I was thinking of putting on a pageant about Michael Harper's high school days. I know he and Tommy were good friends.'

'I'm not sure that would be a good idea,' said Mrs Montag. She smiled. 'It would be hard to capture Tommy's personality in a pageant.'

'What was he like?' Jake asked. 'We're trying to get a rounded picture of him.'

'They have a photograph of him up in the school with his senior class,' said Mrs Montag. 'Haven't you see it?'

'Yes,' said Jody. 'I think my brother meant it more as a metaphor. We want to know more about Tommy.'

'Nobody's asked about Tommy in a long time,' said Mrs Montag. She smiled an odd, sad smile. 'We never heard from Tommy after the fire,' added Mrs Montag. She looked as if she wanted to cry. Then she seemed to pull herself together.

'He was always a difficult child, I have to admit,' said Mrs Montag without any sentimentality. 'Today they might call him "hyperactive". We just called him a little devil. He couldn't sit still, and he was always playing his little jokes.'

'What little jokes?' Jody asked, trying to sound as casual as possible.

'Tommy used to drive me crazy, but I miss him, and I wish I knew where he was and if he's all right,' said Mrs Montag, and she smiled nervously again. 'I was always finding salt in my sugar bowl and sugar in my salt shaker. Then there was the Saran Wrap. I wish they had never invented the stuff.'

'Saran Wrap?' asked Jake.

'It's very hard to see a over a toilet bowl,' said Mrs Montag with a smile. Jake had to look away to keep from laughing. Jody coughed and kept her eyes down in her lap. She knew that if she caught Jake's eye she would start to giggle.

'It was quite disgusting,' said Mrs Montag. 'But we never could convince Tommy of that, no matter how hard we tried, and we did try.'

'What did you do to punish him?' Jody asked.

'We used to lock him in his room,' said Mrs Montag. 'Unfortunately, Tommy was always very good at getting out. He would just climb out the window and go to his friend's house. Then they would both play another joke on my husband and myself. It was very upsetting.'

'Was Michael Harper the friend who helped him escape?' asked Jake, wishing Mrs Montag would stop smiling at inappropriate moments.

'Oh, no. Michael didn't become *good* friends with Tommy until high school. Tommy's best friend was little Buddy Appleton, at least until Tommy and Michael started to play music together. Then they seemed to leave Buddy out more and more.'

'I see,' said Jody. 'I'm sorry, Mrs Montag. This must be very painful for you, remembering Tommy when you haven't heard from him in so long.'

'Oh, no,' said Mrs Montag. 'It's not painful at all.' Jody stared at her. She had a feeling Mrs Montag was lost in a world of her own. Jody found her very creepy, and she began to feel some sympathy for Tommy Montag. He must have started playing practical jokes just to get some response out of his mother. Anything would have been better than her weird, false smile.

'Would you mind if we asked you just a few questions about when Tommy ran away?' Jody asked.

'Oh, no, not at all.' She smiled. 'Would you like another glass of iced tea, or soda, or a cookie?'

'No, thank you,' said Jody and Jake in unison.

'Well, what do you want to know about Tommy running

away?' asked Mrs Montag, getting up and pouring herself a glass of tea. She took a big bite of a cookie.

'Did you make an extensive search for him?' Jody asked.

'Oh, my, yes. We called the police. But there are thousands of runaways about Tommy's age. He was just seventeen when he ran away, and the police said so many kids Tommy's age run away, they couldn't give us much hope. They said unless Tommy decided to return home by himself, there wasn't much they could do. They did ask for all kinds of details about Tommy's looks so they could wire other police departments around the country. But except for his long hair, which he could have cut, Tommy was very average looking. He didn't have any scars or anything outstanding that the police could use to identify him. The only thing I could tell them was that he was terribly allergic to cats. He would start sneezing if he so much as looked at a cat. That was really his only special identifying characteristic . . . that and his practical jokes.'

'You never heard anything from him after he ran away?' asked Jody. 'Not even a postcard?'

'Not a word,' said Mrs Montag. 'I often do wonder how he's doing. He's probably playing jokes wherever he is.' She smiled again.

16

RHYME ON A DIME

Jody thanked Mrs Montag for her time, and then she and Jake walked back out into the sunshine. They unlocked their bicycles in front of Mrs Montag's house. Jody noticed a taxi take off from the kerb opposite from where they had parked their bikes. Jake was shaking his head.

'Did that woman give you a funny feeling?' he asked.

'Very,' said Jody. 'It was as if she was lost in another world.'

'I know,' said Jake. 'I felt as if I was talking to her through a fog.'

'She gave me the creeps,' said Jody. 'She wouldn't stop smiling.'

'I know. I wanted to wipe that smile off her face,' said Jake.

'You know, chimpanzees smile when they're nervous,' said Jody. 'In animals, smiles are often signs of submission. An animal sort of bares its teeth to show it's not going to bite a stronger animal. I read somewhere that people who smile a lot are often very nervous and insecure. You've got to admit,' said Jody, 'nothing she said disproves my theory. If Tommy is back in town, he might not want to see his mother.'

'What next?' asked Jake.

Jody glanced at her watch. 'We've got almost an hour

before we have to meet Bud. I'd like to find out more about Bud Appleton.' She looked thoughtful. 'Don't you have an Appleton in your class?'

'Frank Appleton,' said Jake. 'I don't know him very well.'

'I wonder if he's Bud Appleton's brother,' said Jody.

'I don't know,' said Jake. 'I never made the connection before. I guess they could be.'

'Do you know where he lives?' asked Jody.

'I think somewhere near here,' said Jake.

'Maybe Frank Appleton knows something that could help us,' said Jody. 'Sometimes little brothers are very observant.'

'Thanks.'

'I said "sometimes",' said Jody. 'You're the exception. Seriously, I read somewhere that younger brothers or sisters often know more about older siblings than vice versa.'

'I do know more about you than you do about me,' said Jake. 'So, I'm not an exception. I'm glad to know I'm normal.'

'I wouldn't make any bets on *that*,' warned Jody. 'Let's look up the Appletons' address.' They rode their bikes to a phone booth and found the address in the phone book. Jake had been right. Frank Appleton lived right around the corner from the Montags.

Jody and Jake rode their bikes to the Appleton house and locked them to the picket fence that surrounded the house. Frank Appleton himself opened the door. He seemed surprised to see Jody and Jake. He didn't have many friends at school, and Jake didn't know him well.

'What do you want?' he asked sullenly.

'Is Bud Appleton your brother?' asked Jake.

'Yeah,' said Frank. 'Why do you want to know?'

'This is my sister, Jody,' said Jake. 'She's the one who wrote to Michael Harper and arranged for Michael to come back for the benefit.'

'I know,' said Frank. 'I heard about the concert.'

Jody watched Frank Appleton carefully. He seemed very

resentful. He wasn't nearly as good looking as his brother. He had small eyes, whereas Bud's eyes were huge, and Frank's hair looked dirty and unkempt.

'Did you know Michael Harper before he became famous?' asked Jody.

'He's not so famous any more,' sneered Frank. 'He was just a flash in the pan. Michael Harper is a loser, if you ask me. And so's my brother. They're both losers.'

'What about Tommy Montag?' asked Jody. 'Did you know him before he ran away?'

'Sure, I knew him,' said Frank, his eyes lighting up for the first time. 'I used to think Tommy was the coolest guy in the world. Even though he was older, he always had time for me,' said Frank. His voice became more lively and animated as he talked about Tommy. 'Tommy was great! He used to put chewing gum on our doors . . . things like that . . .'

Jody caught Jake's eye. 'A laugh a minute,' she said dryly.

'It was,' said Frank. 'Nobody does stuff like that anymore.'

'Wrong,' said Jake flatly. Frank looked at him curiously.

'Tommy used to play a lot of jokes with the telephone too,' said Frank. 'I used to eavesdrop. He and Bud would call up strangers and ask, "Is your refrigerator running?"'

'And when they'd answer yes, Bud would say, "You'd better go after it; it's running down the street."' Jake finished Frank's sentence for him.

'Hey, that's right,' said Frank excitedly. 'Did you used to do that, too?'

'When I was nine years old,' said Jake. 'I outgrew it.'

'Well, Tommy was *very* funny,' said Frank defensively.

'A comic genius,' said Jake softly.

Frank ignored him. 'Tommy was different from anybody else I ever knew. He always let me hang around when Buddy and Michael tried to get rid of me. Tommy was even nice to me after he and Buddy had their big argument.'

'What did they argue about?' interjected Jody. She wanted

to steer the conversation away from a listing of dumb practical jokes.

'When they got into high school, Michael and Tommy started to write songs together, and Buddy felt left out,' explained Frank. 'Michael and Tommy told Bud his songs were dumb, and they wouldn't use them in the band. Michael could be very mean when he felt like it. He was always very cocky. He used to really razz Bud about how bad his songs were. Now Michael is eating crow because he writes songs with my brother. Did you know that?'

'Yes,' Jake said, 'only I didn't know Bud was writing songs way back in high school.'

'Bud dropped out of high school,' said Frank. 'He told my parents he could write better songs if he got some experience.'

'Sounds like a dumb reason to drop out to me,' said Jody.

Frank shrugged his shoulders. 'Nobody ever called Bud smart. But he's done okay for himself. Have you seen that Jaguar he drives? Why are you so interested in all this stuff, anyhow?'

'I was thinking about doing a pageant about Michael Harper's days at Shady Brook before "The Joke's on Me" became a hit.'

'I don't know if that's a good idea,' warned Frank. 'I always thought there was something fishy about "The Joke's on Me".'

'What do you mean?' asked Jody.

'Well, Tommy used to write the words and Michael did most of the music. Tommy could make anything rhyme. He could rhyme on a dime.' Frank Appleton grinned. 'Anyhow, Tommy and Michael always used to work together, but then when the record company bought "The Joke's on Me", Michael Harper got all the credit.'

'But by the time the record came out, Tommy Montag had disappeared,' said Jake. 'The record came out after the fire at the stadium.'

'Yes,' said Frank. 'But if he wrote that song, he deserved the credit.'

'You're right,' said Jody thoughtfully. 'Thank you. You might have helped me a lot.'

Frank looked at her, perplexed. 'If you ask me, Tommy Montag was the only one of the three worth anything.'

'Have you seen Bud at all since he came back to town this time?' Jake asked.

'Yeah. He lowered himself to make a visit. He came over yesterday afternoon for a while. He acted peculiar, though. He wasn't really interested in us.'

'Was your brother upset when the stadium burned down and Tommy Montag disappeared?'

'I think I was more upset than Bud was,' said Frank. 'Not about the stadium, but about Tommy. It was a great joke he pulled, and then the stupid stadium had to go and burn.'

'The two were directly related,' Jody reminded him. 'Anyhow, I hope you're planning on coming to the concert to rebuild the stadium.'

'I'll be there,' said Frank. 'I like to hear Michael sing my brother's songs. But I bet you'll have a lot of empty seats.'

'You won't win that bet,' said Jody. 'It would be a stupid bet.'

'It wouldn't be the first I've made,' said Frank.

Something clicked in Jody's mind. 'Your brother likes to bet, too, doesn't he?'

'Bud?' said Frank. 'He's a walking disaster when it comes to gambling. He should join Gamblers Anonymous. He loves to bet.'

17

A WILD RIDE

The road from the Appleton house to the down-town motel where Michael and Bud were staying was mostly downhill. Jody and Jake were travelling too fast to talk comfortably to each other, and Jody used the time to try to sort everything out in her mind.

She felt that an important piece of the puzzle was still missing. Even if Tommy Montag had returned, why had she been attacked at the stadium? Practical jokes were one thing, but the attack at the stadium had been much too vicious to be considered an ordinary practical joke. Jody remembered the feel of the blanket over her head, and she shivered. The bicycle trembled beneath her. Jody decided to slow down. She pressed her hand brake. Nothing happened.

As the bike gained momentum, Jody pressed harder. She could feel the brake digging into her hand, but the bike refused to slow down. Jody concentrated on controlling the bike as it took a curve. She stuck her foot out to slow herself by friction, but it was hard to keep her balance. Jake was a few feet ahead of her, riding up in front because he normally rode faster than Jody. Jody caught up to him and passed him.

'Hey, slow down!' yelled Jake. 'There's a lot of traffic ahead.'

'I can't slow down!' yelled Jody. 'Something is wrong with my brake!'

'What?' yelled Jake. But Jody sped past him before she could answer.

The wind was whipping around Jody's head so fast that she could hear nothing except its roar. She glanced to her left and right, trying to figure out a way to slow down. The curb was too high for her to jump it at this speed. She looked ahead. A stoplight had just turned red. Jody knew she wouldn't be able to stop. She turned right into a steady stream of traffic.

'Why are you turning?' screamed Jake. But Jody didn't even slow down or turn around. 'What is she doing?' Jake asked himself aloud. 'That's not the way to the motel.' Jake was a much more skilled bike rider than Jody, and he used his ten speeds to the best advantage. He hadn't yet had to use his hand brakes. But he pressed on them now to slow down to make the turn, and he experienced the same shock as Jody. His brakes didn't work, either! Jake cursed under his breath. His bicycle wobbled on its thin wheels as he tried to bring it under control. His heart pounded. A car behind him honked furiously, but Jake couldn't stop. He heard the car's brakes screech.

'You stupid kid!' yelled the driver. Jake couldn't stop to explain that it wasn't his fault. He heard the sound of squealing brakes up ahead of him. He only hoped that Jody hadn't had an accident. Jake was going so fast that tears had formed in the corners of his eyes. He couldn't take his hands off the handlebars to wipe them away.

Meanwhile, up ahead Jody *had* narrowly averted having an accident with a car. She realised that her smartest move would be to find a street that went uphill. She looked to her left and right. No streets ran uphill, but the driveways of all the houses sloped up. Jody turned into one, then steered her bike onto the lawn and came to a stop.

Jake followed her, but he had too much momentum and he

wound up in a prickly rose bush. Jake picked himself up out of the rose bush. His forearms were all scratched and he had a scratch on his cheek.

'Are you all right?' Jody asked. She had managed to come to a halt unscathed.

'Yeah,' huffed Jake, out of breath. 'I guess so.'

Jody examined her bicycle. Jake's bike was still entwined in the rose bush.

'My brakes didn't work,' said Jake. 'I gather the same thing happened to you when you passed me.'

Jody nodded her head. 'It couldn't have been an accident – not if it happened to both of us.'

'These stupid practical jokes are getting awfully dangerous,' said Jake angrily. 'We could have really gotten hurt. In fact, I am hurt.' Jake examined the scratches on his arms.

'Look at this!' exclaimed Jody. She pointed to a cut wire leading from her brake to the wheel. 'Somebody *did* cut our brakes!'

Suddenly an elderly man came out and stood on his front porch looking enraged. 'Hey! You kids! What are you doing?' He shook his finger at Jake. 'You deliberately rode right into my rose bush! I saw you!'

'Nobody in his right mind would *deliberately* ride into a rose bush,' said Jake.

'My brother didn't mean to ride into your rose bush,' said Jody quickly. She could tell from Jake's tone of voice that he was not in the mood to be patient. 'We had an accident,' continued Jody. 'We had to use your driveway to stop.'

Jake looked at the rose bush which had his bike ensnared in its brambles. Only one rose had been smashed. 'Believe me,' said Jake, 'I wasn't aiming for them. Look, I'm terribly sorry.'

'I'm going to call the police,' said the man.

'Come on, Jody,' whispered Jake, 'let's get out of here.'

'Maybe we should offer to pay for his rose bush,' whispered Jody.

'It's one rose, not a bush,' said Jake through clenched teeth. 'When I get my hands on the person who snapped my brakes, he or she can pay.' Jake loved his ten-speed bicycle even more than he loved his most comfortable pair of running shoes.

Gingerly, Jake lifted his bicycle out of the rose bush. He looked up at the old man. 'Mister, I'm sorry about your rose bush.'

'Sorry!' shouted the man. 'You young kids are never sorry!'

Jake shrugged his shoulders. The old man went back inside his house, slamming the door behind him.

'That's me,' said Jake, 'the mad rose bush killer. Let me tell you, the rose bush came out better than I did.'

'I don't know,' said Jody. 'You came out smelling like a rose.' She laughed. Jake looked at her.

'Don't tell me you're developing a sense of humour,' he said.

'You're not the only one in this family who can make jokes,' said Jody.

Jake and Jody walked their bicycles down the hill side by side. Jody seemed lost in thought. 'It was such a stupid thing to do,' she said finally.

'I agree,' said Jake. 'The next time I am definitely going to aim for a petunia patch. Petunias don't fight back.'

'I'm not talking about the rose bush,' said Jody. 'I'm talking about cutting our brakes.'

'It could have gotten us killed,' said Jake.

'No,' said Jody. 'It was more of a prank just to annoy us. If somebody wanted to kill us, there are more efficient ways than cutting a bicycle brake. They couldn't know we'd go directly downhill without trying our brakes.'

'Yeah,' said Jake, 'and I guess they couldn't have known I'd head for a rose bush.'

'So what's the point of all these jokes?' asked Jody.

'Well, if you play practical jokes, there doesn't have to be a point,' said Jake. 'That's why practical jokes make everybody so mad. People who play them just think it's funny to annoy other people. After all, what's the point of putting sugar in a salt shaker?'

'There has to be a point to all these incidents,' said Jody. 'I'm convinced there's a pattern, only we don't see it.'

'A practical joker doesn't have a logical mind like you do,' said Jake. 'People who like to play practical jokes just like to know they can make other people feel foolish. They don't even have to be around to watch. It's even to know that something is *going* to happen.'

'It's a cowardly kind of joke,' said Jody.

Jake nodded in agreement. 'But the person who plays the joke feels that he or she has a lot of power. The practical joker likes to pull invisible strings.'

'I'm going to find out who's pulling those strings,' said Jody. She looked grim.

18

A GENIUS WITH THE MIND OF A TWO-YEAR-OLD

Jody and Jake dropped their bikes off at the repair shop down town where they usually took their bikes and walked to the motel. For a second Bud Appleton seemed surprised to see Jody and Jake. He opened the door to his motel room holding a guitar.

'What happened to your face?' he asked Jake, pointing to the scratches on Jake's face.

'I had a little fight with a rose bush.'

'The rose bush won,' said Bud, laughing.

'You're right,' said Jake. 'Only it wasn't particularly funny. I could have been killed.'

'I didn't mean to laugh,' said Bud quickly. 'Come on in. You can wash up.'

He held the door open. Bud gestured for them to sit down on the couch. Jody sat down and jumped right back up again. The couch had made a farting noise. Bud laughed embarrassedly. He reached under the loose pillows of the couch and pulled out a 'whoopee' cushion.

'Sorry,' said Bud, smiling. 'When you're on the road as much as Michael and I are, you get pretty juvenile. I didn't realise Michael had left that cushion there.'

'Are you trying to tell us that's Michael's idea of a joke?' asked Jake.

'Nobody said you had to be mature to be a rock star,' said Bud. 'I'm sure you're discovering that for yourselves.'

Jody sat back down on the sofa, carefully. This time it didn't make any rude noises. 'Tommy Montag loved to play practical jokes, didn't he?' said Jody.

'Now there's a good example of a genius who also had the mind of a two-year-old.'

'So far, nobody we've talked to has called Tommy Montag a genius,' said Jody. 'A lot of other things, but not a genius.'

'Then you haven't talked to anybody about his music,' said Bud.

'Well, your brother said he could rhyme on a dime. He also said that Tommy and Michael left you out once they started writing together.'

Bud played with his moustache. 'Kids can be cruel,' he said. 'But I knew even then that Tommy was someone special. He could have been the greatest if he hadn't run away. Almost everyone thinks they could write a hit song if only they had a chance, but it's not as easy as it seems. Tommy was something else. If he hadn't run away, he might have been another Bob Dylan.'

'But,' said Jody, trying to think of a way to put it delicately, 'Michael hasn't had a hit in a long time.'

Bud didn't say anything. Jody decided to forget the delicate approach.

'In fact,' she said provocatively, 'Michael hasn't had a hit since he began collaborating with you, has he?'

Bud looked angry. 'Michael hasn't *tried* to put our songs across,' said Bud plaintively. 'And he needs me. Michael has always needed a collaborator.'

'But "The Joke's on Me" was his own song, wasn't it?' Jody was deliberately trying to provoke Bud. She had a gut feeling that the authorship of 'The Joke's on Me' was a crucial matter. Perhaps if she could get Bud angry enough, he would reveal something about the strange intertwined relationships among the three – Michael, Tommy and Bud.

'Without my help, Michael might never have written another song,' said Bud, rising to Jody's bait.

Jake realised what Jody was doing. He decided to add to his own contribution.

'That's not true,' said Jake. 'He wrote a song the other day. Apparently he got the idea while he was running. It's called "Hooked on the Past". Michael was very excited about it.'

Bud seemed so angry that the skin around his temples turned white. 'Michael will never finish that song.'

'Why?' asked Jody. 'Don't you want him to write again?' she asked softly.

'He can't write on his own,' said Bud with finality, as if he were pronouncing a sentence. 'Take my word for it, Michael couldn't write himself out of a paper bag.'

'That doesn't sound like a manager talking,' said Jody almost in a whisper. As soon as she said it, she realised she had gone too far. Bud seemed to pull himself together as if he just realised how much he had revealed.

'I'm sorry,' said Bud. 'You're right. It's just that Michael's been so hard to get along with lately. I'm edgy. Not about your concert. I'm worried about Michael.'

No one said anything for several seconds. Jody waited, hoping that if the silence stretched out Bud would reveal more.

Bud stretched his legs out in front of him. He seemed to be back in perfect control 'I guess you're finding the world of rock music isn't a very nice one,' he said.

'I'm not sure it's rock music that's to blame,' said Jody.

'You've had a hard time with this concert, I'll give you that,' said Bud. 'Look, instead of giving you a cheque this time, why don't I give you the five hundred dollars in cash? I have it here.'

Jody stared at Bud in surprise. She had begun to formulate a theory that Bud was behind the practical jokes as a way to get out of paying the cheque. But now that Bud had offered her five hundred dollars in cash, Jody knew she would have to kiss that theory good-bye. *Oh, well,* Jody thought to herself, *theories come cheap.*

Out loud she said, 'Getting the cash would be terrific.'

'Well, we don't want the concert to be a total disaster, do we?' said Bud cheerfully. 'If it goes well, it would be good for Michael. And what's good for Michael is good for me.' He got up to go to his dresser. Someone knocked at the door. 'Who is it?' Bud hollered.

'It's Michael.'

'Not now!' yelled Bud. 'I've got company.'

'Open up,' said Michael. 'You and I have to talk.'

'Later,' insisted Bud.

'It can't wait!' demanded Michael. He pounded on the door. Bud glanced at Jody and Jake. 'I told you, he's been acting crazy. He's keyed up.' Bud went to the door. Michael almost fell into the room. He looked distraught. The circles under his eyes seemed even more pronounced now than before.

'What are you two doing here?' he demanded of Jody and Jake.

'Bud was going to give us five hundred dollars in cash for the printer,' said Jody.

'Oh,' said Michael. He seemed almost in a state of shock. He pulled at his hair the way he had the first night Jody and Jake had met him. 'I'm sorry,' he mumbled. He sank down onto the couch.

Bud took out an envelope from the dresser. He handed it to Jody. 'Here. Hold onto this. I can't stop payment on cash.'

'I'm taking it over to the printer right away, and Jake's coming along as my bodyguard.' She looked over at Jake, as if for confirmation.

'How are we going to get there?' asked Jake. 'Our bikes are not exactly available.'

'Oh, I forgot!' cried Jody. She turned to Bud. 'Can you drive me over to the printer? It'll only take a few minutes. Then you'll know your money is safe.'

Jody had had no ulterior motive in asking Bud, but to her surprise he turned a deep red. 'Uh . . . my car . . . it's broken down,' he stammered. 'It's in the repair shop. It might take them a month to fix it.'

'What happened?' asked Jake. 'That car was such a beauty.'

'Oh, a part broke, and they have to send away for a replacement.'

Michael seemed bored by the conversation about Bud's car and about the money for the printer.

'I'll drive them,' he said impatiently. He turned to Bud. It's hard to imagine you without your fancy wheels for a while.'

'I'll survive,' said Bud.

Michael gave him a disdainful look. 'Come on, Jody,' he said.

'I'm coming, too,' said Jake. He wasn't about to let Jody off alone with anyone connected with the concert.

Michael looked at the envelope in Jody's hand.

'You'd better count it,' he said.

Bud bristled. 'Do you think I would short-change her?' he asked, sounding very insulted.

'I just know that every time she's come near that five hundred dollars, she's got into trouble,' said Michael.

'That's true,' agreed Jake.

'I'd better count it,' said Jody quickly, 'just to be on the safe side.' She glanced at Bud. 'Don't be insulted.'

Jody opened the envelope. She had never seen such a thick wad of bills in her life.

'It's in twenties,' said Bud. Jody counted it as fast as she could.

'Five hundred dollars,' she said, smiling.

'I told you,' said Bud. 'You'll get your posters.'

'She and the school are going to get more than that,' said Michael. 'They're going to get a new stadium.'

Jake thought he seemed awfully confident that he was going to get a crowd.

'Wait for me, Bud,' said Michael. 'I'll drive them to the printer's. When I get back, you and I are going to have a long talk.'

Bud looked grim. He put his arm around Jody and guided her to the door. 'Be careful of him,' he whispered. 'He's in a dangerous mood. Don't let him get you alone.'

19

OUR SONG

Mr Mitford, the printer, seemed shocked to actually receive cash.

'I thought you crazy kids would cancel that order,' he said. 'I've never seen such confusion.'

'Well, now that you have cash, can we have the posters right away?' Jody asked.

Mr Mitford counted his money again. 'Well, I guess you do deserve a little break since you offered me cash. I can have them for you by tomorrow.'

Jody smiled with relief. Finally, at least something was going right.

'I guess you never did find your wallet,' said Mr Mitford. He sounded almost glad, because if Jody had found her wallet, he might have to revise his gloomy outlook on life.

'No,' she said. 'But you have your money, and the posters will be ready. That's the important thing.'

'It certainly was a strange way to have your wallet stolen,' mused Mr Mitford. 'I think about it every time I drive to work.'

'I don't think you have to worry that it will happen again,' said Jody. Michael seemed to be listening to her very carefully. He had been almost completely silent on their drive to the printer's.

Jody and Jake hopped back into the pick-up truck, said goodbye to Mr Mitford, and Michael drove away.

'Shall I take you home now?' he asked politely.

'If it's not too much trouble,' said Jody. 'We went to see Mrs Montag today,' she added softly. She wanted to see what kind of a reaction Michael would give.

He looked startled. He stared at the road for several seconds. Finally, he said. 'Tommy's mother was a very strange lady.' Michael's voice was very gentle, as if he were afraid that if he spoke too harshly something terrible would happen. 'I often think that half the reason he ran away was because he couldn't stand living at home.'

'The other half was that he set fire to the stadium, wasn't it?' said Jody.

Michael nodded. He looked miserable. 'Poor Tommy. It honestly was an accident. I think I was the last person to see him before he ran away. We met right after the fire. He was as horrified as anybody that the stadium burned down. He was so thankful that nobody got hurt, but he was scared. He couldn't face anybody. He had meant it just as a joke.

'People didn't believe me, but I didn't know anything about the joke until it happened. The joke was meant for me. Tommy knew I'd be down on the football field, and we used to fool around and imitate the principal's wife singing "The Star-Spangled Banner". Tommy thought it would be so funny if our song came blaring out of the loud-speakers instead of her voice. He crossed the wires, and it would have been a great joke if one of the wires hadn't been loose and set off sparks.'

'You said "our song",' said Jody. 'On the record, it says that you wrote it by yourself.'

Michael turned and stared at Jody. Jake wished he would keep his eyes on the road. 'That was just a slip of the tongue,' Michael stammered.

Michael banged his hand hard against the steering wheel. Jake jumped. Michael steered the pick-up over to the side of the road and brought it to a stop. Jake breathed a sigh of relief.

Michael turned in his seat and faced Jody and Jake. 'I might as well tell you. I plan on telling everybody at the concert. I've been lying about "The Joke's on Me". Tommy and I wrote that song together. I never meant to steal the credit from him, but after he ran away, a few months later a record producer approached me about making a demo of the song. I didn't tell the producer that half the credit belonged to Tommy. I told myself that Tommy wouldn't mind, that he didn't want to come out of hiding. But I lied to myself and to everybody else.'

Michael's words were coming out in a rush, as if he couldn't get them out fast enough. 'When our song became a hit,' he continued, 'everyone told me what a great songwriter I was. I just couldn't confess. I took all the glory, and I've been feeling miserable ever since. I couldn't face coming home until I got Jody's letter. Then I knew that I wanted to come home and face the music.'

Michael screwed up his face. 'I never could resist a bad pun. Tommy used to tease me about that unmercifully. Basically, I used to write the music and Tommy would do the words, although we'd help each other so much we never knew where one person's idea ended and another's began. I wish he were here to help me with "Hooked on the Past". I've got a melody and a refrain, but I need him to help me with the verses. I don't want Bud to touch this song.' Michael sounded bitter.

'Why did you start writing songs with Bud?' Jody asked.

'I was so low,' answered Michael, 'I felt I needed somebody. And there was Bud. So I gave him a chance.'

20

JODY'S LISTS

It was just seven days to go until the concert. The sale of the tickets was going well, and there had been no more incidents. Jody should have been pleased. Instead, she was pacing up and down the kitchen floor while Jake tasted his tomato sauce. He smiled and added a bit more oregano. 'You're going to wear out the linoleum,' said Jake.

'I'm mad at myself,' snapped Jody.

'You don't have to take it out on me,' said Jake. 'Why are you mad at yourself?'

'Michael's explanation left too many questions unanswered. We never found Tommy Montag. We never found out who attacked me at the stadium.'

'It had to be Tommy Montag,' said Jake. 'He'll come out of hiding when he hears how much money is waiting for him. You can ask him then.'

'I'm not so sure it was Tommy Montag,' said Jody. 'I've made another list. Wait here.'

'I'm not going anywhere,' said Jake. 'Remember, my bike's broken. Besides, this sauce needs a lot of care.'

Jody ran out of the kitchen and came back waving a piece of paper in the air. She began to read from her list:

- chewing gum on the door
- posters got ruined

- cheque No. 1 gets stolen when I stop for fake body
- blanket over the head at the stadium
- cheque No. 2 missing
- bicycle brakes tampered with

'That's quite a list,' said Jake. 'Maybe you can win a list-making contest with it.'

'Be serious,' said Jody. 'Does Michael's explanation cover any of those things on my list?'

Before Jake could answer, Jody answered her own question. 'No!' she shouted, so loud that Chico and Groucho both jumped off the kitchen counter.

'No,' agreed Jake, in a much softer voice.

Jody leaned over the kitchen counter. 'Are you agreeing with me to stop an argument?' she asked.

'No,' said Jake. 'A lot of things don't make sense. Do you think Michael really was in touch with Tommy Montag and told him you were supposed to meet him at the stadium?'

'No,' said Jody thoughtfully. 'I think Michael was telling the truth as far as he knows it. I don't think Michael knows where Tommy Montag is.'

The doorbell rang. Jody and Jake looked at each other.

'Your turn,' they said in unison. Then they both laughed.

'This is stupid,' said Jake. 'I cook. You open the door.'

'I open the door twice as much as you do, anyway,' complained Jody.

'You're twice as curious,' said Jake. The doorbell rang again. 'You'd better get it.'

Jody gave him a mock-dirty look and went for the door. A cab driver stood at the door looking very annoyed.

'Yes?' asked Jody.

'Your cab is here,' snarled the driver.

'I didn't order a cab,' insisted Jody. The driver looked up at the number on the Marksons' house. 'This is 918 Sullivan Street, isn't it?'

'But we didn't order a cab,' protested Jody.

Just then another cab drove up and parked in front of the house. The first cab driver looked at Jody suspiciously. The second cab driver honked his horn. He leaned out of his window and yelled, 'Are you the party who ordered the cab?'

'No,' said Jody. 'There's been some mistake.'

'Nine-eighteen Sullivan Street?' asked the cabbie.

'Yes,' said Jody, 'but I didn't order a cab.'

Jake came to the door. 'What's going on?' he asked.

The first cab driver got into his cab and slammed the door shut. 'It's a dumb joke! You kids, you're so funny. Well, you are a little old to be playing these kind of jokes. The next time you order a cab, you can whistle for it.' The second cab driver slammed his door and drove away, too.

'It looks like the mad practical joker is on the prowl again with his silly jokes,' said Jake.

Jody didn't answer him. She seemed completely lost in thought.

'Get me my list!' Jody ordered.

'On the double,' said Jake.

'I didn't mean to order you around,' said Jody, 'only you just gave me an idea when you said "silly jokes". In fact, you gave me another idea just now when you said "double".'

'Would you mind sharing some of those ideas with me?' said Jake.

'All along there have been two kinds of practical jokes: the chewing gum, the phone calls – those that didn't hurt anyone. Then there were the malicious jokes – the fake body, the incident at the stadium, tampering with our bikes.' Jody got out a pencil and paper and wrote:

Practical	*Malicious*
• chewing gum	• fake body
• phone calls	• incident at the stadium
• cab drivers	• tampering with bikes

She stared at the two lists. 'I'm convinced that the jokes are being done by two different people. Look at my list, Jake.'

Jake peered over her shoulder at the different lists. 'What do all the jokes on the second list have in common?' she asked.

'I don't know,' said Jake slowly. 'You said it yourself. The jokes on the second list are much more nasty than the jokes on the first list.'

'There's something else,' said Jody. She sounded very excited. Chico and Groucho were playing with a ball of yarn on the floor. Jody watched them for a while and then her eyes lit up. 'We're going to set a trap,' she said, grinning.

'Why are you smiling at Chico and Groucho?' asked Jake. 'They're very cute, but . . .'

'What was the one special identifying characteristic Mrs Montag gave the police to help them identify Tommy?' Jody asked.

'He was allergic to cats.'

'Right,' said Jody. 'I have a feeling that Tommy Montag has stayed very close to everyone connected with the concert. My first job is to bring him out of hiding. Then we'll find out which set of jokes he is responsible for!'

'Which one do you think?' asked Jake.

'I can make a guess,' said Jody, 'but I don't want to tell you yet. I could be wrong. I've got to make some calls. I want to check on exactly what was wrong with Bud's car.'

'Why?' asked Jake.

'I'm not sure it really is in a repair shop. I've got an idea about what Tommy could have done with his car.'

'Don't be so mysterious,' said Jake, scowling.

'Don't look at me like that,' said Jody. 'We're going to clear up all the questions very soon. I'm sure of it.'

'Exactly how are you going to lure Tommy Montag into the house so he can start sneezing?' asked Jake.

'We're not,' said Jody. 'We're going to bring Chico and

Groucho to him.' Jody picked up Groucho. He purred contentedly.

'Would you mind explaining?' asked Jake. 'Or is that another of your secrets?'

Jody smiled. 'No. In fact, you have to know about this because you're playing an important part – you and Groucho and Chico.' Harpo wagged his tail by her feet. 'We have to leave you out, boy,' said Jody, patting him on the head. 'But you did your job when you found me in the stadium.'

'Well,' said Jake, 'would you tell me what you're planning?'

'It's simple, really,' said Jody. 'I have a feeling that Tommy Montag has stayed very close to everyone connected with the concert. If we let everyone know we're having a rehearsal at the stadium, he'll show up.'

'He's not going to sneeze in a huge stadium,' objected Jake, 'even if we do hide Groucho and Chico there.'

'No,' smiled Jody, 'but he would in the locker room. I know how small that room is. I've spent hours there. Come on, I've got a lot of setting up to do.'

21

THE SET-UP

'You mean I'm finally going to meet Michael Harper?' Robie shrieked over the phone.

'The rehearsal's at five this afternoon,' answered Jody. 'You and everyone who's worked on the committee will be there.'

'This is not going to be a very intimate introduction,' said Robie sadly.

'I promise you,' said Jody, 'it will be intimate enough.'

'But the whole world knows about the rehearsal,' complained Robie. 'I was listening to the radio and the deejay announced that Michael Harper would be having his first rehearsal at Vickers Stadium today.'

'Well,' said Jody, 'we need all the publicity we can get. I'll find a time to introduce you to Michael personally. I'll meet you at the stadium.' Jody hung up. She smiled to herself.

'You seem to have things under control,' said Jake, coming into the room.

'I wouldn't say that,' answered Jody. 'However, I think it's time to get Groucho and Chico into their boxes.' Jody searched under the couch and found Groucho's and Chico's favourite catnip toys. She put them in their boxes.

'I hope you've explained to them that it's for a good cause,' said Jake.

'They won't be in their boxes any longer than they would if

we were taking a trip,' said Jody. 'And I even bought them each a new catnip toy.' Jody took out two identical catnip mice from a brown paper bag and put the new toys in the boxes. Groucho and Chico both crept up on their boxes to sniff the toys, and Jody left the boxes open so that the cats would have time to become used to them.

'What are you going to do when Tommy hears them mewing?' asked Jake.

'Well, you're in charge of keeping them fairly quiet,' said Jody. 'You'll be with them all the time, and the sound of your voice should calm them down, plus the smell of you. I don't expect them to be too nervous. Secondly, Michael's backup band will be practising. That should drown out some of the noise.'

'You think of everything, don't you?' said Jake.

'I'm not sure,' said Jody. 'I'm scared. A lot could go wrong. I'm calling Mom.' Jody picked up the phone. Mrs Markson sounded anxious when Jody told her they were going to the stadium to watch Michael rehearse, and then Jody told her mother the rest of her plan.

'Are you sure you'll be all right?' asked Mrs Markson. 'We never found out who it was who attacked you.'

'I think we're going to settle it this afternoon,' said Jody. 'I just wanted to let you know what we're planning, in case anything goes wrong.'

'I don't like the idea of you and Jake going to the stadium alone,' said Mrs Markson.

'We'll hardly be alone,' said Jody. 'I've taken care of that.' Jody spoke to her mother for several minutes. Then her mother spoke and Jody listened, nodding her head every few seconds.

'Explain this all to Jake,' said Mrs Markson.

'I will,' said Jody. 'Mom, I've got one last question. If the person who was responsible for the fire in the stadium confesses now, would he or she still be liable for arson? It happened two years ago.'

Mrs Markson thought for a moment. 'It has been only a few years. He or she could still be charged, but I am sure it was never arson. Arson is setting a fire deliberately. This was an accident, wasn't it?'

'Yes,' said Jody.

'At the worst, it would be "malicious mischief", but if the person didn't have a previous record, a good lawyer should be able to get him or her off with probation.'

'Thanks, Mom. I know where the person can get a good lawyer,' said Jody. She hung up the phone.

Jake was pacing up and down in the living room. Chico and Groucho were playing with the catnip toys in their boxes.

'How did you plan on getting to the stadium?' he asked.

'We'll have to take a cab,' said Jody. 'We have to sneak Chico and Groucho in without anyone noticing. But I've got a sign that will make their boxes look like their equipment for Michael's band.'

Exactly,' said Jake. 'We have to call a cab. Don't you remember that little prank one of your jokesters played? I bet they won't come to our address. They'll think it's another joke.'

'You're right,' said Jody. 'I didn't think of that. You'd better call the cab company.'

'Why me?' asked Jake.

'Make your voice sound low. Maybe they'll take you seriously.' Jody handed the phone to Jake.

'You're older,' said Jake, stalling. 'You'll sound more mature.'

'Jake, call the cab company,' ordered Jody.

Jake reluctantly picked up the receiver. 'Hello,' he said. 'I'd like a cab sent to 918 Sullivan Street, please.'

'Is this a joke, sonny?' said a gruff voice. So much for sounding mature, Jake thought. 'We've had just about enough of you.'

'We didn't have anything to do with the joke,' pleaded

Jake. 'If anything, we were the victims. But we honestly need a taxi. We'll pay for it.'

'I don't know,' said the dispatcher. 'You sound like the person who called us before.'

'No, I'm actually Jake Markson, and we live here. We need a taxi.'

The dispatcher seemed to think for a moment. 'Give me a number where I can call you back. If it checks out in the directory to be the Marksons' number, I'll call you back.'

'Fine,' said Jake. He gave the dispatcher their number and hung up.

'We have to wait for him to call us,' Jake explained to Jody. 'He's looking our number up in the phone book to see if it checks out.'

'I hope he doesn't look it up under "Mud",' said Jody. 'We don't want to be late.' She paced the room nervously.

The phone rang. It was the taxi dispatcher.

'Yes, it genuinely was us who called for the taxi this time,' said Jake. He hung up. 'The taxi will be here in a few minutes,' he said.

'Let's get ready,' said Jody.

'I feel we should go armed with a "whoopee" cushion and a dribble glass to meet this creep.'

'We're armed with Groucho and Chico,' said Jody. She made sure Chico and Groucho were inside their boxes, and then she gently closed the lids. She carried the boxes to the hall.

'We've got to be careful,' said Jody. 'Remember, there are still a lot of unpredictable things that could happen.'

'You don't have to warn me,' said Jake. 'You're the one who doesn't have the sense to be scared.'

A car honked.

'It's the taxi!' shouted Jody.

On the drive to the stadium Jody was unusually quiet. As the taxi turned into the parking lot of the stadium, Jody felt her heart begin to race. Jake was wrong. She was scared. All the terror of those hours spent locked up in the stadium returned. Jody shivered involuntarily.

'Are you all right?' asked Jake.

Jody nodded. 'It's just that I don't like this place,' she said.

22

THE CAT TRAP

The gate by the box office was open. Jody spotted Michael's pick-up, and several other vans, but there was no sign of Bud's Jaguar. Jody and Jake could hear electronic squawks coming out of the loudspeaker system.

'At least there isn't that eerie silence,' said Jody.

'Let's just hope Bud doesn't sing one of his songs,' said Jake.

They walked through the stadium and out towards the stage. Jake was carrying the cat boxes made up to look like pieces of equipment for the band. Michael and several other members of his band were on the stage, shifting around various microphones. Michael waved to Jake and Jody and spoke into the microphone.

'Glad you got here,' he said. His voice bounced around the stadium. Jody and Jake felt extremely small walking along the field, looking up at the stand.

'I wonder where Tommy Montag is,' Jody whispered. 'I know he's around here somewhere.'

Jake nodded. 'Maybe he's hiding somewhere with a blanket over his head.'

'It's time for you to go into hiding with Groucho and Chico,' said Jody. 'Good luck. I'll be down to check out your hiding place in a few minutes.'

Jake turned and headed for the locker room.

Jody walked across the field alone. She drew closer to the stage. She saw Robie and a bunch of other kids from the committee in charge of the concert. She waved to Robie.

Bud was moving around the stage changing wires. He was drinking a diet soda. Michael was tuning his guitar. He smiled at Jody.

'Hi,' said Michael, pausing in his guitar-playing. He leaned down from the stage. 'Want to come up here? Everyone wants to pretend they're a rock star, once.' Michael held out his hand to Jody.

Jody clambered up onto the stage. She looked out into the mostly empty stands. Michael was right. She had an irresistible urge to grab a microphone and strut up and down the stage as if she were a rock star.

'It's intoxicating, isn't it?' said Bud. He held out his can of soda. 'Do you want a sip?' he asked.

'No, thanks,' said Jody.

'Why do you drink that poison?' asked Michael.

'I have to watch my weight,' said Bud. He handed Jody a microphone. 'Bet you can't sing all the words to "The Joke's on Me",' he said.

'No bets,' said Jody. She jumped as her voice went out over the stadium. She hadn't realised the microphone was turned on. Robie laughed when she heard Jody's voice.

Jody handed the microphone back to Bud. She suddenly remembered why she was here. 'Excuse me,' she asked Michael, 'can I talk to you for a second?'

Michael walked her to the edge of the stage.

'What's up?' he asked.

'There's something important I have to say to the key figures in the concert,' said Jody. 'It's very important. Can we hold a meeting in the locker room in a half-hour?'

'Sure,' said Michael. 'Why all the big secrecy?'

'Oh, it's not a secret,' said Jody quickly. 'In fact, it's just the opposite. You could save me a lot of time if you'd announce the meeting over the microphone. I don't know where Jake is, and my friend Robie should be there. Could you announce over the microphone that there is an important meeting?'

'Sure,' said Michael. He looked at her strangely. 'Are you positive that's all? You seem very nervous.'

'Just make the announcement,' said Jody nervously. 'Here's the list of who should be there.'

Michael gave her a puzzled look, but he walked up to the microphone. 'I have an announcement,' he said. 'We have to hold an important meeting about this concert in the locker room on the lower level. Will Bud Appleton, Jody and Jake Markson, and Robie Harris all meet with me in the locker room in fifteen minutes? Thank you.'

'What's this meeting about?' Bud asked sharply, coming up behind Jody.

'It's something we have to get settled before the concert,' said Jody. 'I'll see you in the locker room.'

Jody ran down the steps through the stadium to the locker room. She knocked on the door three times.

'Enter. It's the cat man,' whispered Jake.

'Michael made the announcement,' said Jody. 'Get ready.' Jake was standing in a dark corner of the locker room. The old blanket that had been used to tie up Jody was next to him. Chico and Groucho were still in their boxes. They mewed softly.

'Are they okay?' whispered Jody. 'I didn't want to have to put the blanket over them until the last minute.'

'What about me?' said Jake.

'Shh!' said Jody. 'We don't have much time.' Jody flung the old blanket over Jake and the boxes containing the cats. She walked to the centre of the room. Jake looked as if he was nothing but a pile of old blankets and sports equipment abandoned in the locker room.

'Perfect,' said Jody.

'Easy for you to say. It's dusty in here,' mumbled Jake.

'You're telling me. I was tied up in one of those, remember? How are the cats?'

'Fine,' whispered Jake. 'You'd better get out of here.' Jody ran out of the locker room.

Twenty-five minutes later, Jody walked into the locker room with Robie, Michael Harper, and Bud Appleton.

'Michael Harper,' said Jody, 'I want you to meet Robie Harris.' Robie smiled shyly and held out her hand.

'Did you bring us down here to this dusty locker room just to make introductions?' snapped Bud impatiently.

'No,' said Jody. 'This locker room seemed a fitting place to hold a meeting since I spent such an unusual afternoon here.'

'What is this about?' demanded Bud.

Jody scanned the oversized lockers surrounding the wall.

'There was a number of things I thought should be cleared up,' said Jody, stalling for time. 'I have a couple of lists with things I thought we should discuss.' Jody dug into her jeans pocket and came out with her list of practical jokes.

'Where's Jake?' asked Robie. 'Wasn't he supposed to be here?'

'He's around,' said Jody.

Suddenly someone sneezed.

'God bless you,' said Robie to Michael.

'I didn't sneeze,' said Michael.

'I didn't, either,' said Bud, looking mystified.

'Who sneezed?' demanded Robie.

Another loud sneeze filled the small locker room. Jody walked over to the lockers in the direction of the sneeze. She opened the lockers. The first two were empty. She opened the third one and a tall, thin blond boy grinned at her with the most impish grin Jody had ever seen.

'Oh, no,' he said softly in a scared voice. 'I guess this time the joke's on me.'

23

THE SODA FIGHT

'Tommy!' yelled Michael. He practically grabbed Tommy out of the locker and hugged him. Tommy grinned sheepishly.

'Where are the cats?' he asked.

Jake emerged from his pile of blankets in the corner, holding Chico and Groucho.

'Take them outside, Jake,' said Jody. 'I think Tommy Montag has suffered enough.'

Jake put the cat boxes right outside the locker room door and went back in.

'How did you know I was allergic?' asked Tommy.

'Your mother told me,' said Jody. 'I figured you must have heard about Michael's concert on the radio, and you returned out of curiosity. It must have hurt you to have to listen to "The Joke's on Me" when it was a hit. You knew you had written the words, but you got none of the credit.'

'I swear, Tommy,' said Michael, 'I'm so glad to see you. I was going to come clean at this concert. You can ask these kids, Jody and Jake, or ask Bud. I was going to give you all the credit you deserve, and your money, in the hopes that you would come out of hiding.'

'The cats accomplished that,' said Tommy dryly.

'And Jody Markson,' said Michael, 'this was a great idea.'

'I'm not so sure,' said Tommy. 'As soon as the cops find out that I was the one who started the fire, I'll have to go to jail.'

'You probably won't have to go to jail,' said Jody. 'I checked with my mother, who's a lawyer, and she thinks at the most you'll probably get probation.'

'But what about the tricks he played on you, Jody?' asked Michael. 'Will *you* press charges?'

Tommy Montag looked shocked. 'I admit I put chewing gum on your door, and a few other stupid jokes, but I don't think I did anything criminal to you. I found out by calling the school that Jody Markson was in charge of the concert. I sneaked over to the school to find out what was going on. I admit I spilled the red paint on the posters. I got furious when I saw Michael's picture because I knew I had written the words for "The Joke's on Me', and I thought, *I would have been famous, too, if I hadn't pulled that dumb joke at the stadium.* Then, I also didn't want the concert to go on, but I couldn't think of a good way to stop it. I did follow Jody home, and I put chewing gum on the door, and I made some silly phone calls, mostly to find out if Jody was home, and to disguise my voice. I tried to think up a way to stop the concert, but my mind went blank, so I just tried to keep up with what was happening. I didn't really have any plan in mind.'

'But somebody had a plan to stop Jody,' said Jake. 'Who tied her up in the stadium?'

'I wouldn't do anything like that!' cried Tommy, looking astonished.

'There have always been two jokesters,' explained Jody. 'That's what made it so confusing.' She turned to Bud, who had started to back up toward the door. 'Would you like to make any bets about who was responsible?' she asked.

'What are you talking about?' snarled Bud.

'One set of jokes were relatively innocent,' said Jody. 'The other set had a purpose. A joke was played on me every time I had a cheque until finally you gave me cash. I began to suspect that the jokes were just camouflage for the fact that there never was any money in yours or Michael's bank account to cover the cheque. Michael told you I was taking the cheque to the printer. You knew the road to the printer's was deserted. You set up the trick with the fake body and waited for me. But then when I asked you for another cheque, you couldn't say no – so you pulled the blanket over me in the stadium to get the cheque and to get me to drop out of arranging the concert. You played those jokes on me in order to get the cheque back. You knew that everyone would suspect that Tommy Montag was back in town. They would blame him. I have a feeling that if Michael goes over his books, he will discover that you've been stealing from him.'

Bud put his soda down on a bench. Jody was standing between him and the door. He shoved her viciously and tried to run out the door.

Michael jumped in front of him and grabbed his arm. 'I suspected something when you kept avoiding me when I wanted to go over the books,' said Michael. He turned to Tommy. 'I had made up my mind to put your half of the money in an account for you and use the rest to rebuild the stadium. I told Bud I was going to do that at the concert.'

Jody turned to Michael. 'When you gave me a blank cheque, I should have realised that you had no idea how to keep track of money. You made it so easy for Bud to steal from you, he couldn't resist the temptation – especially for a person who loves to gamble the way he does. Bud's only hope was to try to get the cheque back. But he didn't want to arouse your suspicions. He trapped me in the stadium partly to get the cheque back, but also he hoped that I would get fed up and stop working on the concert. Then he could convince you to cancel, and he hoped that everything would go on as before. When that didn't work, he finally resorted to selling his Jaguar to raise cash. I called every repair shop in town, Bud, and no one has brought in a Jaguar to be repaired. But one shop told me that they had bought a Jaguar recently.'

'You little brat!' Bud practically spat the words out. 'You've been nothing but trouble ever since you wrote that dumb letter to Michael. I should have done more than just tie you up in this locker room.' Bud lunged for Jody.

'Bud!' yelled Michael. Bud swung around, his hand balled into a fist. He looked furious, almost as if he could kill. They began trading blows. Tommy Montag tried to pull them apart, but he got flung into the lockers for his efforts. Robie shrieked.

'We've got to stop them!' yelled Jody. She grabbed Bud and tried to prise him away from Michael, but Bud shrugged her aside as easily as he had Tommy.

Bud and Michael fell fighting to the floor. Bud was on top, landing several blows on Michael.

'Stop it!' shouted Jody.

'That was great,' whispered Jake. 'Very effective.'

'Do something,' said Jody. 'I'll go call the police.'

'Wait a second,' said Jake. 'Hand me Bud's diet soda.'

'I've had enough of your jokes,' warned Jody.

'I'm serious,' said Jake. 'Give it to me.' Jake took the diet soda. He circled the fighting men. As he walked, he kept shaking the can of soda up and down.

Bud was still on top. Jody could see the strain on Michael's face as he tried to push Bud off.

'Michael's getting hurt,' whispered Jody. Jake circled the fighters so that he was directly behind them. Then he held his finger over the top of the can and continued shaking it up and down. Sweet, gooey, sticky spray squirted in all directions.

Bud wiped his eyes. Michael lay on his back, heaving. Jake gave the can another shake and squirted Bud again. Bud turned on Jake in a fury and tried to grab the can away from Jake, holding Jake's wrist in an iron grip.

Suddenly the door opened and Mrs Markson rushed in, followed by the policeman and policewoman who had questioned Jody before.

Bud dropped Jake's wrist and tried to run out of the locker room, but the policewoman grabbed him and made him stand against the wall.

24

'HOOKED ON THE PAST'

'How did the police get here?' Michael asked in astonishment. Tommy had turned white and he seemed to try to hide himself in a corner.

Jody smiled at her mother. 'We had a back-up plan in case our trap with Groucho and Chico didn't work, or in case there was any violence. At six o'clock, Jake and I were to call Mom and use the word "spaghetti" in the conversation. We knew that would be easy for Jake. "Spaghetti" is our code word for "all clear".'

Mrs Markson examined Jake's wrist. He shook it and reassured her he was all right. 'Jody knew that if I didn't hear from her by six o'clock, I would come to the stadium with the police. If I had heard from her and she had not used the word "spaghetti", I would assume she was being forced to make the phone call, and I would have come to the stadium, anyhow.'

'It sounds like a complicated plan,' said Michael. 'But it worked. Bud might have run away if you hadn't got here.'

Bud turned and glared at Jody and Jake. 'It's all your fault. If you hadn't interfered, Michael would never have found out how much money is missing.'

'He's probably right,' said Michael. 'I paid so little attention to the money, I had no idea how much I was making.'

'You don't have much left,' said Bud viciously.

'I think we had better remind you of your rights,' said the policeman. And he read Bud the list of his rights as an accused person. Then the police took Bud to the station house.

Michael watched him go. Tommy Montag was still standing in the corner, a sad expression on his face. Michael turned to Tommy. He looked equally sad.

'I keep feeling it's all my fault,' said Michael. 'Bud was always the scaredy cat of the three of us. Bud always used to be afraid of our pranks because he thought we'd get in trouble. But that was when we were little.'

Tommy nodded his head. 'I don't think Bud ever grew up. We used to tease him all the time, and we would leave him out, especially when we started our music. I guess we used to be pretty mean.'

Michael sighed. 'Then, when I let Bud become my manager and write songs with me, I think he got a taste of power. He couldn't let go. It's all my fault.'

'You're going to drive *yourself* crazy if you go on feeling so guilty,' said Jody.

'But I am,' said Michael.

'You're guilty of not giving Tommy credit,' said Jody. 'But you had already decided to do something about that. And Tommy's here, so you can do something about it right now.'

Michael grinned at Tommy. 'I've needed you. Singing those stupid songs that Bud wrote, I felt like such a fool. I've missed you.'

'I didn't like being invisible,' said Tommy. 'Running away was pretty miserable. I felt like I didn't know who I was. I missed working with you, too.'

Mrs Markson coughed. 'I spoke to the police informally about the charges against you for the fire at the stadium. I have a feeling that if you explain to them how it was an accident, you will be able to get off with just probation.'

'You can do more than explain,' said Michael excitedly. 'You can give the concert with me. Together, we'll raise enough money to rebuild that stadium. We have six days left. We can put together a great programme.'

Tommy smiled shyly. 'Okay,' he said, grinning. 'Only, put an expert in charge of the wiring. I don't ever want to have another accident like that again.'

The last days before the concert went by like a whirlwind for Jody. She could never believe there could be so many details to take care of. She and Jake and Robie were exhausted by the night of the concert, but thrilled, too. Because of the publicity surrounding the return of Tommy Montag, and the news that Tommy and Michael would be singing together, the concert had sold out.

Jody and Jake stayed backstage, watching the show from the wings. Michael and Tommy stood on the platform. Michael grinned. He stepped up to the microphone.

'Ladies and gentlemen . . . I can't tell you how happy I am to be back home.' He hit a chord on his electric guitar and the crowd went wild. 'Some of you recognised that chord as the opening note from "The Joke's on Me". Well, tonight the joke *is* on me. My best friend, Tommy Montag, is going to come out here because that song belongs to him. He wrote the words. I wrote the music, I've lied to you. Tommy, get out here.'

Tommy practically flew onto the stage. His long blond hair was perfectly clean and it shone in the spotlight. He grinned at Michael.

'I've got a confession to make. Two years ago, I played a silly joke and I irresponsibly burned down the stadium. I was just lucky that nobody got killed. And I took the coward's way out and ran away. But just like Michael, I'm glad to be back.' Tommy hit the opening chord on his guitar.

'All right!' shouted Michael. 'You people didn't come here to hear our confessions. You came to hear music.' Tommy and Michael hit their electric guitars simultaneously and went into the best version of 'The Joke's on Me' anybody had ever heard. When it was over, the crowd went wild.

Both Michael and Tommy were covered with sweat. Michael held out his hand to quiet the crowd. 'It is *great* to be back!' he shouted. 'Now, we would like to sing you a new song, one that we just finished writing together. We'd like to dedicate it to two kids, Jody and Jake Markson. They taught us that living with the truth, no matter how frightening, is better than living a lie, especially if the lie belongs to the past. This song is dedicated to Jody and Jake.'

Michael and Tommy played a haunting chord progression. Then they sang 'Hooked on the Past'.